'Grapefruit Juice and Sugar'

Bold Quilts Inspired by Grandmother's Legacy

By Jenifer Dick

Kansas City Star Books

Acknowledgments

You can't truly know the magnitude of writing a book like this until you begin—then you find out how much you need people. So many people generously provided information and quilts for this book. I want to thank them all—without them this book would still be an unfulfilled dream.

- First and foremost, to Shirley Bockelman for loaning grandma's patterns to me. I can't tell you how much these patterns have meant to me. Without them, I would have never gotten to "know" my grandmother.
- To Mom and Dad, Audrey and Donald Bockelman, for supporting me no matter what, and answering all my endless questions patiently and willingly. Also, for generously allowing the quilts to be photographed at their home.
- To Darlene Metsker for allowing me to incorporate the family history and research from her book into mine.
- To Carol Bockelman, and Sue and Paul Bockelman who answered my many questions and shared their stories of Grandma.
- To grandma's children who so generously loaned their quilts for inclusion in the book: Darlene Metsker, Allen and Shirley Bockelman, Donald and Audrey Bockelman, and Carol Bockelman. To Danny Smith, grandma's grandson and Darby Rusher, grandma's great-granddaughter who also loaned their quilts for this book. And to Paul Beisel, Phylis Bockelman and Julie Henderson, who shared information about their quilts and their memories of Grandma with me.
- To the quiltmakers who dropped everything to make quilts that appear in the book: Denniele Bohannon, Debra Fieth, Mariya Drechsel and Dianne Barnden. To the long-arm quilters who squeezed in the quilts to get them done in time: Dana Davis, Sherri Dolly, Lisa Winkler, Brenda Weien and Denise Hester. Also, to the women of the United Methodist Quilters in Harrisonville, Mo. The year I spent on the waiting list was worth it!
- To Sheila Reece and Yvonne Poor, who did anything I asked of them, not the least of which was to sew sleeves on quilts.
- To Kathy Brandes, former owner of Kathy's Quilts Plus in Harrisonville, Mo., who let me teach when I had never taught before. Because of you I have the experience and confidence to do something crazy like writing a book! I'll always appreciate your generosity and friendship.
- To Connie Read, owner of Heritage Fine Fabrics in Belton, Mo., whose support and fabric helped create many of the quilts in this book.
- To the editorial and design team at **Kansas City Star Books**, whose professionalism and expertise made this project come to life: Vicky Frenkel, Krissy Krauser, Jo Ann Groves, Doug Weaver and Deb Rowden. Deb, your guidance and calm demeanor have been an inspiration.
- And, especially to my husband, Ray, and children Abe, Nate and Ellie, who lived in the "trenches" during the writing of this book and endured many sandwiches and hot dogs so I could work "just a little bit longer" on the book.

'Grapefruit Juice and Sugar'

Bold Quilts Inspired by Grandmother's Legacy
Author: Jenifer Dick

Editor: Deb Rowden
Technical Editor: Jane Miller
Designer: Vicky Frenkel
Photography: Krissy Krauser, with assistance by Rebecca Friend
Illustration: Jenifer Dick and Gary Embrey Design/Eric Sears
Production assistance by Jo Ann Groves

Published by:
Kansas City Star Books
1729 Grand Blvd.
Kansas City, Missouri, USA 64108

First edition, first printing
ISBN -13: 978-1-933466-01-4
ISBN -10:1-933466-01-9

Printed in the United States of America by Walsworth Publishing Co., Marceline, Mo.

To order copies, call StarInfo at (816) 234-4636 and say "Books."

PickleDish.com

The Quilter's Home Page

TABLE OF CONTENTS

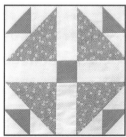

Dena L Goosman Bockelman (1900-1977) about 1974. Photo by Sue Bockelman.

About the Author

Jenifer Dick has been quilting for more than 12 years and teaching for the past three. She is a member of the Log Cabin Quilter's Club in Harrisonville, Mo., and the Blue Valley Quilt Guild in Overland Park, Ks.

She has won several quilting awards at county- and state-level competitions.

She received a bachelor's of journalism degree from the University of Missouri in 1989 and worked as a magazine editor and graphic designer before leaving work to stay home to raise her family.

Jenifer lives in Harrisonville, Mo., with her husband and three children. She considers herself to be a dedicated quilter, meaning it's more than a hobby, it's a lifestyle. She sews on a quilt, designs a quilt or teaches quilting to someone every day.

Dedication
To Ray, without whom nothing is possible.

About this book

Every quilter will someday leave behind her collection of patterns, tools, fabric and, of course, quilts. Many collections will be sold or given away—or worse, unappreciated. We are fortunate if we have someone who will cherish these treasures as much as we do.

This is the story of how I discovered my Grandmother's quilts and patterns 25 years after her death, and how I grew to love a woman I never really had the chance to know.

About the patterns

The Kansas City Star newspaper published **Pine Tree**, the first of 1,068 quilt patterns, on September 19, 1928. It's likely that on September 20, 1928, the first **Kansas City Star** quilt pattern collection was begun. In a day when quiltmaking books and magazines were in limited supply, women all over the Midwest must have eagerly awaited the paper each week to get their free pattern.

I chose these nine *Kansas City Star* patterns to create new quilts because of their names, their beauty—and because they were ones my grandmother thought enough of to save. However, many of the original patterns are not practical to use by today's standards. Some have errors, some are designed to finish in awkward sizes and none have rotary cutting instructions. I have updated them for today's quiltmaker.

Although several of the quilts in this book are appropriate for quilt makers of all levels, many are geared more for the quilter who has made a few quilts and would like to take his or her skills to the next level. For basic quiltmaking instructions, look for one of the many basic quiltmaking books at your local library or quilt shop.

How to use this book

You'll find information on various aspects of quiltmaking and some special instruction that will help you make the quilts in the *How to use this book* section, which begins on page 122. Check the end of each chapter for helpful tips.

Grandmother's Legacy

This book is about the influence **The Kansas City Star** quilt patterns have had on two generations of quilters in my family—my grandmother and myself. And it is through these precious patterns that I got to "know" the grandmother I never had the chance to know in life.

My Grandmother

I have only a few memories of my grandmother. She died when I was 10 years old, and as one of 22 grandchildren, I suspect she never knew me either. Because I was so young when she died and because she wasn't an influential force in my young life, I never really thought about her or what her life must have been like. But that all changed when my aunt, Shirley Bockelman—grandma's daughter-in-law—loaned me two spiral notebooks full of **Kansas City Star** quilt patterns Grandma saved throughout her life. It wasn't until I pored over these little beautiful gems that I realized how much Grandma and I had in common. We both had a shared love of quilting that affected our lives profoundly and deeply.

My quilting life

I began quilting when my children were little. My oldest was almost three, the next was 14 months old and I was pregnant with my third. Around this time, my sister-in-law Sharon Bockelman made a quilt. I watched and decided I could make a full-size quilt for my oldest child. He needed a quilt for his "big boy bed" and I needed something to do besides being a mom. I had taken a beginning quilting class five years

before, so I knew the basics and was overly confident that I could do this in the four months before baby number three joined our family.

When I was born, my parents began collecting dollhouse furniture and paraphernalia in anticipation of the day I was old enough to play with them. When I was 7 years old, my parents decided I was responsible enough to play with the toys without breaking them. Dad hadn't yet made the dollhouse, so I played with the furniture on the Grandmother's Flower Garden quilt made by Grandma. Each of the "flowers" was a room and the sashing between the flowers was the hallway of my pretend dollhouse.

For the next few months, I carefully cut out the pieces of fabric while the boys were napping, and sewed them together by hand while they were playing and after they went to bed. It only took about three months to piece the top. I knew I couldn't hand quilt it before the baby came, so I tied it and hand-quilted it around the borders. It certainly was not an award winning quilt, but I finished it and my son loved it. Of course this quilt led to the next and the next. In all, I made four quilts in the next two years. I certainly was hooked.

I reveled in a hobby that took me away from my responsibilities for a little while each day. Although raising children and keeping house is what I wanted to do, it was hard to leave my job as a magazine editor and graphic designer. I missed the creativity of my former work and the professional accolades it brought. But when I made that first quilt, I felt something inside that was so freeing and joyful— I knew this is what I wanted to do for myself.

Grandma as a quilter

As I made my first quilts, several family members mentioned that Grandma Bockelman made quilts too. My mother, Audrey (grandma's daughter-in-law), owns three of these quilts and has them displayed in her house.

I learned from other family members that Grandma made one quilt for each of her nine children. Most of them are the "Double Wedding Ring" pattern, but a few are "Grandmother's Flower Garden." In all, she made at least 17 quilts.

The more I heard, the more I wanted to know about grandma's quilting. I wondered if she would have wanted to talk about her quilts with me. Would we like the same patterns and color schemes? Would we talk about new techniques? I wanted to know, but with Grandma gone, I didn't think those questions could ever be answered. I felt that I missed out by not knowing her. I often wondered what she thought about her quilts and why she made them. And, I hoped she would have approved of my efforts.

Several years after I made my first quilt, my aunt Shirley mentioned she had some old quilting patterns of grandma's and wondered if I would like to see them. She said that no one wanted them when grandma's estate was settled, so she saved them rather than seeing them thrown out.

I had no idea what to expect when I received two three-ring school notebooks. Originally, I only hoped to find the pattern of my Oklahoma's Square Dance quilt made by Grandma sometime in the 1960s. That would have been enough. Instead, I found the insight into my grandmother's quilting that I never thought I'd have.

In 1993, my Aunt Carol Bockelman, Grandma's youngest child, gave me a quilt and matching afghan Grandma made. It was gold, brown and cream—not contemporary colors— but the workmanship and design were good. I never could find the name of the pattern—In fact, at first I couldn't even determine what the block looked like, because of the overall optical illusion of the quilt.

As I looked through the notebooks, there in the upper left hand corner of one page was a little advertisement for a quilt. It was my quilt! Underneath was another copy of the exact same advertisement only on this copy, Grandma colored in the quilt in the same brown and gold that she made the final quilt out of. This is the only quilt pattern in all her clippings that she colored in.

The notebooks were stuffed with page after page of newspaper block patterns glued to wide-ruled notebook paper—110 pages in all, with about 500 different patterns represented. The pattern dates ranged from the late 1920s to 1977. Two hundred fifty one patterns easily identified from

The Kansas City Star were interspersed with as many patterns from **McCall's Magazine, Woman's Day, Woman's Household, The Workbasket, Popular Needlework**, Mountain Mist Batting Co. and numerous other unidentified sources. Some were dated, and some were not. Some were duplicates. Some were familiar-looking with strange, old-fashioned names. Grandma evidently collected every pattern or article that related to quiltmaking she came across.

In addition to the patterns were some blocks she made—samples that never made it to a quilt—and her hand-drawn sketches of blocks she admired. The first time I looked through these notebooks, I was in awe. I had seen a few "authentic" **Kansas City Star** patterns, but never page after page of them. Each was a mini time capsule of twentieth century quilting history. The patterns were in excellent condition—just a little yellowing. The turn of each page was like Christmas morning!

Grandma was a dedicated collector. It appears that she saved almost every newspaper or magazine article she found having to do with quiltmaking. She even saved the wrappers that the batting came in. She glued the patterns to wide rule notebook paper and kept them in two spiral ring notebooks. I'm sure she flipped through them many times imagining the quilts she would make some day.

The names of the blocks she admired made me laugh—so many were appropriate to her life— Contrary Husband, Little Boys Britches, My Little Girl's Dresses, Missouri Star. She seemed to like the blocks that held symbolism for her life. I also am drawn to blocks with names that have important meaning to me at a specific time in my life. It dawned on me that quilters are quilters the world 'round, no matter what era they live!

It wasn't until the initial euphoria wore off and I inspected the patterns closer that I realized that these were many of *my* favorites too! I marveled at how similar our quilting interests were! Coming from a graphic design background, I am intuitively drawn to blocks with strong graphic appeal. Many of these types of blocks were represented in her notebooks: The X Quartette, Goose in the Pond, the Long Nine Patch, Triplet and numerous more. Just like the ones I save, too. It became clear to me that she would have liked my quilts, just as I treasure hers.

My grandmother

Dena Goosman was born Feb. 25, 1900, in Odell, Gage County, Nebraska, to a hard-working, fairly wealthy farming family. In 1908, her family moved to a 280-acre farm near Nashville in Kingman County, Kansas, where she spent the rest of her childhood. She was educated at the town's Lutheran Church, where they spoke and taught in German. When Dena was in the third grade, the pastor/teacher left and the children were moved into the English-speaking public school. This was difficult for Dena. She stopped her formal education after elementary school, as did many of her siblings, to help on the family farm.

In 1919, the family moved to Donna, Texas, (which is about 20 miles east of McAllen) where they had bought a farm sight unseen from a man who turned out to be a swindler. Once there, they found the land unsuitable for farming, as promised. They worked the land for three years, but eventually abandoned the property and bought another farm sight unseen in Chelsea, Oklahoma, which is in the northeastern corner of Oklahoma, just over the Kansas border from Independence, Kansas. This too, was not a successful move, and the family lost everything.

During this time, Dena and her sister Ella worked as maids for wealthy families in Independence, Kansas, and then in Kansas City, Missouri. During a trip to visit her parents in Chelsea, Dena became reacquainted with Arthur Bockelman, a childhood friend from Nashville, Kansas. Arthur had moved to Chelsea with two of his brothers who bought farms there. Dena was dating other men, but Arthur won her heart. During their courtship, he lavished her with gifts, including a black fur coat. They married

on May 20, 1923, and moved to Kansas City, Missouri. Five years later, she saved her first quilt pattern booklet, "Quilt Patterns, Patchwork and Appliqué," published by the Ladies Art Company in St. Louis, Missouri.

Dena spent all of her adult life in and around Kansas City, raising nine children and keeping house. In addition, she amassed her collection of quilt patterns. The last pattern she collected was dated April 17, 1977. She died one week later on April 24.

Someone snapped this shot of Grandma while she was on the phone in the early 1950s.

During her child-rearing years, Dena made tied comforters. These were largely utilitarian quilts, probably used to keep the family warm. These were made on her treadle sewing machine and tied on her quilt frame.

Dena and Arthur Bockelman, shown here about 1923. Grandma sports the fur coat that Grandpa gave her while they were courting. Grandpa made such an impression on Grandma that she gave up her other suitors for him. Could the fur have had anything to do with that? The marriage survived 50 years, but no one knows what happened to the coat.

Grandpa, who was a builder by trade, made Grandma's quilt frame sometime in the early 1960s, probably using a pattern from The Workbasket magazine. Although time and use has taken a toll on it, it's not hard to imagine all the quilts that were both tied and hand quilted on this frame.

It is unlikely that she made any pieced quilts during her first 40 years of marriage. None have survived if she did and none of her surviving children remember her making any. She had a big job just to feed and clothe her brood of nine children during the Great Depression. But she certainly dreamed of quilts and collected all the patterns she could, optimistically planning to make them someday.

Dena's first pieced quilt is signed and dated January 1963—not coincidentally the year her youngest child, Carol, graduated from high school. After spending 40 years raising a family, she was accustomed to being busy. Now, with her domestic responsibilities slowing down, she had time to make her quilts.

This tied quilt is an example of what Dena's early tied comforters may have looked like. This one was probably made by Dena in the early 70s. It is made mostly out of polyester scraps. Darlene, her oldest child, remembers the children helping tie these comforters when she was young.

DENA L. BOCKELMAN
JANUARY 1963

This is the only signature she put on any of her quilts and it's also her first pieced quilt. It's embroidered with her name and the date: Dena L. Bockelman, January 1963.

Her first quilt was a Double Wedding Ring, made with scraps of her boys' work shirts. Unfortunately, it has not held up over time, and in fact, began deteriorating in her lifetime. She told my mother, who now owns this treasure, that she'd never make another quilt with used fabrics. From then on, she either bought new or used new scraps from other sewing projects.

None of her children remember exactly the details of Dena's quilting life. They were all busy raising their own families and living their own lives when she began quilting in earnest. We do know that she probably made 17 quilts between 1963 and 1977, when she died. Nine were for her children. Others were given away by Grandma, or disbursed at the time of her death.

Grandma's quilts today

I now feel a connection to my personal quilting heritage in a way I never have before. These quilt patterns are my legacy—they represent all the quilts my grandma never had the chance to make. But more than that, they also represent a generation of women who had a wonderful resource for patterns that came into their homes every week. How many notebooks must there be in attics all over the country with these wonderful treasures? How many quilts must have been inspired by a little corner of newsprint in their local newspaper? These are part of the quilting heritage of all of today's quilters.

Shortly after the full impact of the meaning of these two notebooks sunk in, I began taking my favorite blocks of her favorites and started doodling with quilt designs. Soon I realized that I was finishing the quilts that my grandmother never had a chance to finish. They became the quilts I hoped to create in my lifetime. Grandma didn't get to make them, but I can make them for her, for myself and for our descendants.

All quilters have a special affection for their scissors and thimble. No tools work harder when making a quilt. Grandma's scissors were given to her by Audrey Bockelman, her daughter-in-law and my mom. Mom couldn't bear Grandma using the inexpensive, dull scissors she had made do with for years. She presented Grandma with these Wiss scissors for Christmas in the late 1960s.

In addition to quiltmaking, Grandma made a variety of crafts, including dolls like this. The clothing this doll wears—a purple velvet and black broadcloth—are scraps from the dress her mother, Sophie Goosman, wore on the honeymoon after her wedding. Grandma also stitched a sister to this doll with scraps from her mother's wedding dress.

Chapter 1

Honey Bee

Combining appliqué and piecing, the *Honey Bee* block is as fun to make as it is versatile. If you prefer another option for the appliqué shapes, then **Bubblegum in the Pantry** will show you how to use embroidery embellishments to make a charming small quilt. The **Do Bees Come Out at Night?** wall hanging uses the traditional appliqué shapes to create the blocks. At the end of the chapter, look for the tip *Embroidery stitches to embellish the Honey Bee block.*

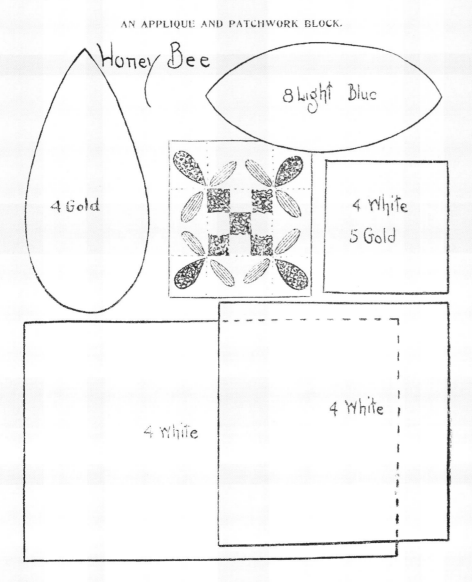

AN APPLIQUE AND PATCHWORK BLOCK.

Honey Bee

8 Light Blue

4 Gold

4 White
5 Gold

4 White

4 White

Honey Bee block—Originally published August 24, 1929. Said The Star:

"The Honey Bee" is a charming example of a quilt design combining the favorite methods of piecing and appliqué. A little nine-patch block is used as the center block of another sort of nine-patch, the other sections of which have appliqué as shown in the small sketch.

As in the other patterns of The Star's *quilt series the patterns given do not allow seams, but should be cut about a quarter of an inch larger all around so the finished parts will be the sizes here printed.*

It is a bit less trouble to piece the entire block first and appliqué the bee's wings and bodies afterward. This is done by creasing a seam width back all around each piece. Basting them carefully placed and then whipping or blind stitching to the white background.

Honey Bee blocks are much more attractive when set together with large, plain white squares the size of this block.

Single block instructions

Honey Bee

Finished block size: 12"

This block is a simple nine-patch with strips of plain fabric surrounding it. Appliqué shapes make the wings and body of the bee. Refer to these instructions when making the two quilts described in this chapter, or make the single block for a sampler quilt.

Fabric requirements

- White: 1 fat quarter
- Gold: 1 fat eighth
- Light blue: 1 fat eighth

Cutting instructions

From white, cut
- 2—3 1/2" x 6 1/2" strips (B)
- 2—3 1/2" x 12 1/2" strips(C)
- 1—2 1/2" x 18" strip, cut into 4—2 1/2" squares (A)

From light blue, cut
- 1—2 1/2" x 22" strip, cut into 8—2 1/2" squares (E)

From gold, cut
- 1—2 1/2" x 22" strip, cut into 5—2 1/2" squares (A)
- 1—3" x 22" strip, cut into 4—3" squares (D)

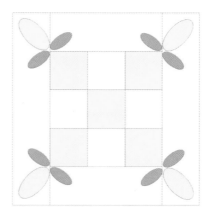

Block Diagram

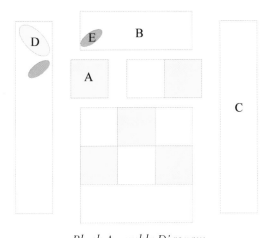

Block Assembly Diagram

Applique shape E

2. Layout shapes on block using the *Block Assembly Diagram* as a guide. Baste the shapes into place and stitch as desired. This block was machine sewn with black thread using a buttonhole stitch.

Piecing the block

1. Make the center nine-patch unit. You'll need 4 white squares (A) and 5 gold squares (A). Lay out as shown in the Block Assembly Diagram. Sew units into 3 rows. Press. Sew the completed rows together to complete the block. Press. This unit should measure 6 1/2".

2. Sew 1 short, white rectangle (B) to either side of the nine-patch unit. Press. Sew 1 long, white rectangle (C) to the top and bottom of the nine-patch unit. Press.

Preparing the shapes for appliqué

1. Refer to *Easy interfacing appliqué* on page 91 to prepare appliqué shapes D and E. You need 4 gold shapes for the body of the bee (D) and 8 blue shapes for the wings (E).

Applique shape D

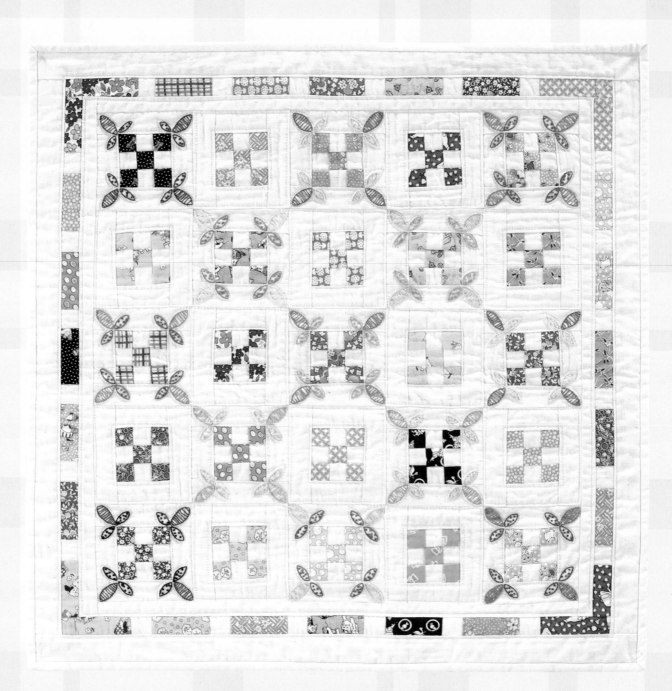

Bubblegum in the Pantry

22" x 22"

Pieced and quilted by Jenifer Dick, Harrisonville, Mo.

Bubblegum wishes

One of the best things about Grandma's house was her pantry. It was actually just a broom closet on the right side of her refrigerator; but it was what was inside that made it magical. Back in the mid '70s, you could get brightly colored bubblegum balls in individually wrapped plastic. These wonderful treats were strung together in long strips. Grandma kept hers in the pantry hung from a nail, well within easy reach of my little hands.

Each trip to Grandma's house began with a flurry of hints about that bubblegum. If she didn't respond, then I'd be a little more bold in my wishes. She probably knew all along what I wanted! After I was told that I could have one, I'd make a mad dash to the pantry, and the treat would finally be mine. How I wish I could find bubblegum like that today.

Bubblegum in the Pantry

Block size: 3 3/8"
This quilt is made of 25 blocks in a straight set with no sashing. It is a true scrap quilt, using up to 25 different fabrics. Embroidery embellishes the blocks. Three borders frame the top: a 1/2" plain muslin inner border; a 5/8" multi-color pieced border; and a 1 1/2" plain muslin outer border.

Fabric requirements
- Unbleached muslin: 1 1/3 yards (includes backing)
- 1930s reproduction fabric: 25 scraps or fat eighths in different colors and patterns
- Binding: 1/4 yard muslin. This allows for 3—2" wide strips to make about 100" of binding. If you prefer 2 1/2" wide strips for binding, purchase 1/4 yard.
- Batting: scrap measuring 25" x 25"

Additional supplies
- Embroidery floss: several shades that blend with the colors used.
- Embroidery needle
- 6" embroidery hoop
- Freezer paper

Blocks

Cutting instructions
From muslin, cut
- 4 strips—1 1/4" wide x the full length of fabric, cut into 50—1 1/4" x 2 3/8" strips (B)
- 5 strips—1 1/4" wide x the full length of fabric, cut into 50—1 1/4" x 3 7/8" strips (C)
- 100—1 1/8" squares (A)
From each print fabric, cut
- 5—1 1/8" squares (A)

Piecing the blocks
To make the 25 blocks, use the directions for piecing the single block found at the beginning of this chapter. *Note:* The pieces are very small for the nine-patch blocks. Take care when sewing, and use an accurate 1/4" seam allowance. Measure the nine-patch to make sure it is exactly 2 3/8" unfinished before moving on to the next step. A small sewing discrepancy at this stage will magnify as the quilt continues to be pieced. *Note:* The honey bee body and wing shapes will be embroidered after the quilt top is assembled.

Borders
Inner border
Using the remaining muslin, cut:
- 2 strips—1" x 17 3/8"
- 2 strips—1" x 18 3/8"

Pieced middle border

Cutting instructions
From muslin, cut
- 24—1 1/8" squares

From 20 different prints, cut
- 1 each—1 1/8" x 2 1/2" strip

From 4 prints different from the 20 above, cut
- 1 each—1 1/8" x 2 1/2" strip
- 1 each—1 1/8" x 3 1/8" strip

Note: Each of the 4 borders has 6 muslin squares and 7 different colored scrap strips. Lay out 6 muslin squares and 7 different print strips for each border. Keep in mind that 2 print strips—1 long and 1 short—of the same color will meet at each of the 4 corners. Make sure when laying out the fabric that you have the correct colors at the ends of the pieced borders. See the *Quilt Top Assembly Diagram* for placement guide. Stitch pieces together into border strips. Press.

To cut the pieced borders accurately, fold each in half and crease the center with your fingers to mark it. Measure the length from the center out and cut a little off each end. The borders should measure:
- 2 short borders—1 1/8" x 18 3/8"
- 2 long borders—1 1/8" x 19 5/8"

Outer border
Using the remaining muslin, cut:
- 2 strips—1 3/4" x 19 5/8"
- 2 strips—1 3/4" x 22 1/8"

Assembling the quilt top
Referring to the *Quilt Top Assembly Diagram*, lay out the blocks. Make sure the color values are spread evenly throughout, with no 2 colors next to each other. Be sure to turn every other block one-quarter turn to avoid matching seams.

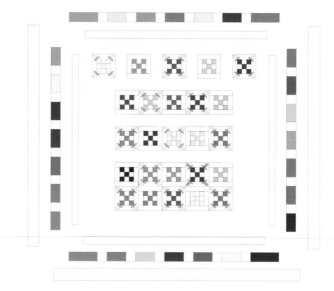

Quilt Top Assembly Diagram

1. Sew the blocks into rows of 5. Press. Join these rows together to make a top with 5 rows of 5 blocks each. Press.

2. Add the short muslin inner borders to the sides of the quilt top. Add the long muslin inner borders to the top and bottom of quilt. Press after each border is added.

3. Add the short pieced middle borders to the sides of the quilt top. Add the long pieced middle borders to the top and bottom of quilt. Press after each border is added.

4. Add the short muslin outer borders to the sides of the quilt top. Add the long, muslin outer borders to the top and bottom of quilt. Press after each border is added.

Embroidering the blocks
1. Because of the small size of this quilt, assemble the entire top before embroidering the honey bee shapes. Only every other block is the Honey Bee block, the other block is a plain nine-patch. Referring to the

Quilt Top Assembly Diagram, determine which blocks need the honey bee shapes embroidered.

2. Mark the entire top. To do this, trace several shapes each of the honey bee body (F) and wings (G) onto the paper side of freezer paper. Cut out the shapes on the drawn line. Lay out the shapes, shiny side down, on the quilt top as they appear in the *Block Assembly Diagram*. This can be done on 1 or 2 corners of each block at a time—it is not necessary to lay out the shapes on the entire quilt at once.

Applique shape F

Applique shape G

Press the shapes in place with a hot iron. Let cool slightly and trace around each shape lightly with a pencil. This will be your guideline for embroidering the shapes. Remove the freezer paper and move to a new area. If the freezer paper begins to wear out, trace shapes onto fresh freezer paper.

3. Choose the colors you want to embroider each block. You can either complement the fabric by using colors that match, or contrast the block by using opposite colors. Don't worry too much about color choice. Because so many colors are used on the top, any colors you choose will blend in and look great. Keep in mind: you might not want to use identical colors in blocks next to each other.

4. Now, embroider. Place the hoop in the center of the top and embroider the middle block first, working your way out. Use two strands of floss about 18" long, and outline stitch each shape. Fill in the shape with any stitch of your choice. The quilt shown uses a loose satin stitch for the body of the bee and French knots for the wings. Refer to *Embroidery stitches to embellish the Honey Bee block* on page 21, for instructions in how to make these stitches. *Note:* Remove the hoop after each sewing session, to keep rings from forming on the top.

5. Press the top before quilting. To do this, lift the iron up and down along the top so not to disturb the embroidery stitches.

Quilting and finishing the quilt

Layer the backing, batting and top. Baste and quilt as desired or use the suggestions below. Once quilted, bind in muslin to match the outer border.

Machine quilting suggestions. Because it is small, this is an easy project to machine quilt. The example shown was quilted with a walking foot and thread to match the muslin. Each plain block was quilted 1/16" from the seam around the nine-patch and around the inner edge of the block. The blocks with the honey bees were echo quilted around each of the honey bee shapes and around the nine-patch. The borders were simply quilted 1/4" from the inner edge of each border.

Hand quilting suggestions. There is not much room for fancy quilting on this project. The quilting pattern should be small scale to complement the small pieces. Stitch in the ditch around each block to stabilize the quilt then fill in with about a 1" cross-hatch grid, skipping over the honey bee shapes. For the borders, stitch the entire inner border in the ditch and sew straight lines down the center of each border.

Do Bees Come Out at Night?

39 1/2" x 39 1/2"

Pieced and quilted by Jenifer Dick, Harrisonville, Mo.

Do Bees Come Out at Night?

Block size: 12"

This quilt is made of 5 blocks set on point with 4 setting triangles and 4 corner triangles. It has 2 borders: a plain red 1" inner border and a plain black 2" outer border.

Fabric requirements
- Black: 3 1/3 yards (includes enough for backing)
- Red: 5/8 yard (includes enough for binding)
- Purple: fat quarter
- Gold: fat quarter
- Turquoise: fat quarter
- Batting: crib size, 45" x 60"

Additional supplies
- Spray starch
- Freezer paper
- Glue stick
- Invisible thread or thread to match appliqué shapes
- Light-colored marking pencil

To get the most of the yardage, cut the following from the **black** fabric and set aside:
- 1 1/3 yards for backing
- 4—2 1/2" x the full width of fabric strips for the outer borders. These will be cut to size later.

Cut the following from the **red** fabric and set aside:
- 4—1 1/2" x the full width of fabric strips for the inner borders. These will be cut to size later.
- 11" for binding. This allows for 5—2" strips to make about 182" of binding. If you prefer 2 1/2" wide strips for binding, set aside 13".

Blocks

Cutting instructions
From black, cut
- 1—2 1/2" x the full width of fabric, cut into 20—2 1/2" squares (A)
- 2—3 1/2" x the full width of fabric, cut into 10—3 1/2" x 6 1/2" strips (B)
- 4—3 1/2" x the full width of fabric, cut into 10—3 1/2" x 12 1/2" strips (C)

From purple, cut
- 2—2 1/2" x 22" strips, cut into 16—2 1/2" squares (A)

From gold, cut
- 1—2 1/2" x 18" strip, cut into 5—2 1/2" squares (A)
- Save the remaining gold for appliqué.

From red, cut
- 4—2 1/2" squares (A)

Piecing the blocks

To make the 5 blocks, use the directions for piecing the single block on page 12. *Note:* There are 2 colorways for the blocks. You'll make 4 with purple and gold nine-patch units (Block A) and 1 with a red and gold nine-patch unit (Block B). Sort fabrics according to colorways, and pay attention to color placement so blocks are stitched correctly.

Block A   *Block B*

Preparing the shapes for appliqué

1. Refer to *Easy interfacing appliqué* on page 91 and prepare appliqué shapes F and G. You'll need 20 gold shapes for the body of the bee and 40 turquoise shapes for the wings.

2. Lay out shapes on block using the *Block Assembly Diagram* as a guide. Baste the shapes into place and stitch as desired.

Setting triangles

Cutting instructions
From black, cut
- 1—18 1/4" square, cut in half diagonally twice to make 4 setting triangles.

Corner triangles

Cutting instructions
From black, cut
- 2—9 3/8" squares, cut in half diagonally once to make 4 corner triangles.

Borders

Inner border
Using the reserved red strips, cut
- 2 strips—1 1/2" x 34 1/2"
- 2 strips—1 1/2" x 36 1/2"

Outer border
Using the reserved black strips, cut
- 2 strips—2 1/2" x 36 1/2"
- 2 strips—2 1/2" x 40 1/2"

Assembling the quilt top
Referring to the *Quilt Top Assembly Diagram*, lay out blocks, setting triangles and corner triangles.

1. Sew 3 Honey Bee blocks together, making sure Block B is in the center. Add 2 corner triangles to each end. Press.

2. Referring to the *Quilt Top Assembly Diagram*, sew 2 setting triangles to either side of Block A. Press. Add a corner triangle. Press. Make 2 of these units.

3. Join the 3 units together. Press.

4. Add the short red inner borders to the sides of the quilt top. Add the long red inner borders to the top and bottom of quilt. Press after each border is added.

5. Add the short black outer borders to the sides of the quilt top. Add the long black outer borders to the top and bottom of quilt. Press after each border is added.

Quilting and finishing the quilt
Layer the backing, batting and top. Baste and quilt as desired or use the suggestions below. Once quilted, bind in red to match the inner border.

Machine quilting suggestions. Using black thread, quilt 1/4" from the inside edge of each block, setting triangle and corner triangle. For each block, quilt around the appliqué shapes and cross hatch the black squares in the nine-patch. In the open areas of the setting triangles and corner triangles, quilt the honey bee shape, centered in the middle.

To do this, trace the honey bee shapes onto the paper side of freezer paper. Cut out shapes on the line. Place on the quilt top, shiny side down, and press. Trace around the shapes with a light colored marking pencil. Remove the freezer paper and stitch on the line.

Quilt the black inner border 1/4" from the red middle border around the perimeter of the quilt. Quilt the black outer border 1/4" from the red border around the perimeter of the quilt.

Hand quilting suggestions. To give the quilt a playful look, quilt whimsical flowers with small garden insects such as dragonflies in the large open spaces. Echo quilt around the appliqué shapes and cross hatch the nine-patch as described above. Cross hatch the borders in a 2" grid.

Tip: Embroidery stitches to embellish the Honey Bee block

For the outline of the honey bee body and wings, use the stem, or outline stitch. Thread an embroidery needle with 2 strands of embroidery floss. Tie a small knot at the end; trim the tail. Bring the needle up through the block to the front on the marked line. Take a small stitch along the line and pull the needle through (Figure 1), making sure your stitches are a uniform length. Keep the thread consistently either above or below the line. End the line of stitches by tying a small knot on the back close to the fabric; trim the tail.

*Figure 1:
Stem stitch*

To fill in the wings, use a French knot. Thread an embroidery needle with two strands of embroidery floss. Tie a small knot at the end; trim the tail. Bring the needle up through the block to the front and wrap it around the needle 3 times (Figure 2). Put the needle just to the side of the entry hole and push through

the wrapped thread, keeping your thumb on the wrapped area so that it will not become loose (Figure 3). Continue filling in the space with as many knots as desired. End by tying a small knot on the back close to the fabric; trim the tail.

Figure 2: French knot 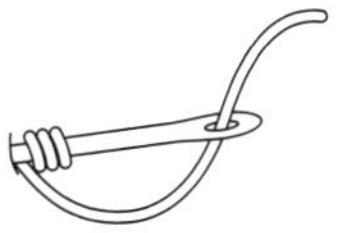   *Figure 3: French knot*

To fill in the body of the bee, use a loose variation of a satin stitch. Thread an embroidery needle with 2 strands of floss. Tie a small knot at the end; trim the tail. Bring the needle up through the block to the front. Make straight stitches to cover the body as shown in Figure 4. Keep the thread flat and smooth. There would be no spaces in between lines in a true satin stitch. In this variation, leave spaces about 1/16" apart. End by tying a small knot on the back close to the fabric; trim the tail.

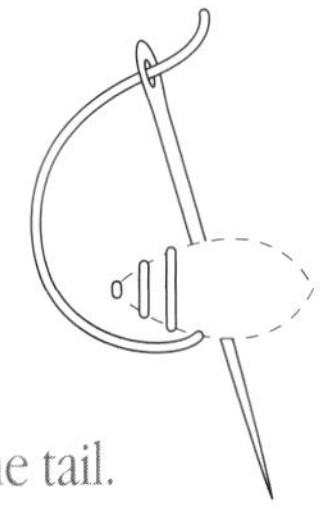

*Figure 4:
Loose satin stitch*

Chapter 2

Missouri Puzzle

Something as simple as setting a block on point can make a dramatic difference in appearance. The *Missouri Puzzle* block featured in this chapter proves that. Our **Zip! There It Goes!** quilt features the block in a straight set, looking quite traditional. The **Fall Star Table Runner** sets the block on point for a more elegant look. You will find a helpful tip, *Making mitered borders*, at the end of the chapter.

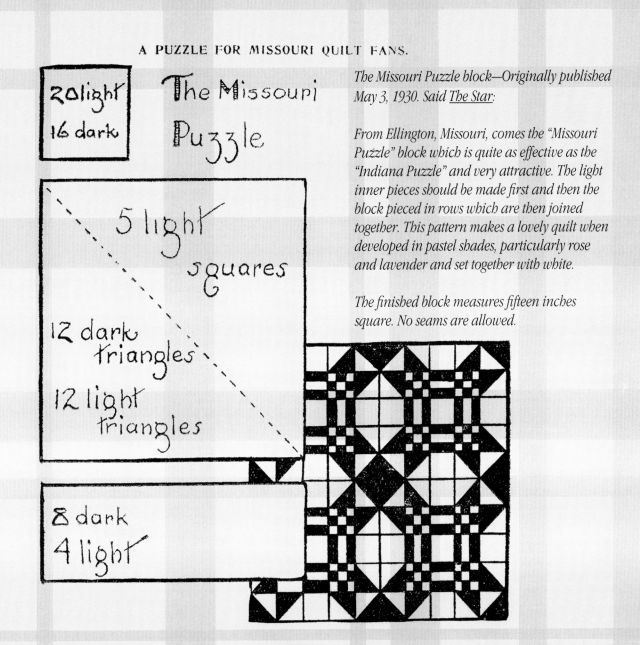

A PUZZLE FOR MISSOURI QUILT FANS.

20 light
16 dark

The Missouri Puzzle

5 light squares

12 dark triangles

12 light triangles

8 dark
4 light

The Missouri Puzzle block—Originally published May 3, 1930. Said <u>The Star</u>:

From Ellington, Missouri, comes the "Missouri Puzzle" block which is quite as effective as the "Indiana Puzzle" and very attractive. The light inner pieces should be made first and then the block pieced in rows which are then joined together. This pattern makes a lovely quilt when developed in pastel shades, particularly rose and lavender and set together with white.

The finished block measures fifteen inches square. No seams are allowed.

Single block instructions

The Missouri Puzzle
Finished size: 15"

This block is constructed as a 25-patch in 3 colors. Twelve half-square triangle units, 4 nine-patch units, 4 strip-pieced squares and 5 plain squares make up the units within the block. Refer to these instructions when making the two quilts described in this chapter, or make the single block for a sampler quilt.

Fabric requirements
- White: 1 fat quarter
- Pink: 1 fat quarter
- Purple: 1 fat eighth

Cutting instructions

From white, cut
- 6—3 7/8" squares (A)
- 5—3 1/2" squares (B)
- 3—1 1/2" x 15" strips (C)
- 1—1 1/2" x 22" strip (D)

From pink, cut
- 2—3 7/8" squares (A)
- 3—1 1/2" x 15" strips (C)

From purple, cut
- 4—3 7/8" squares (A)
- 2—1 1/2" x 22" strips (D)

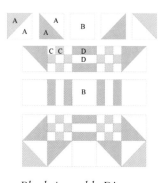

Block Assembly Diagram

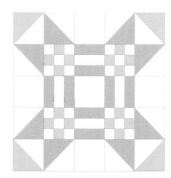

Block Diagram

Piecing the block

1. Referring to *How to make half-square triangle units* on page 45, make 12 half-square triangle

units in 2 colorways using the squares (A). Trim units to 3 1/2".

Make 4 units (Figure 1) using 2 pink squares and 2 white squares. Make 8 units (Figure 2) using 4 purple squares and 4 white squares.

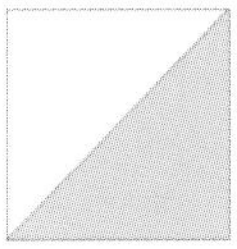

Figure 1   *Figure 2*

2. Make 4 nine-patch units using (C) strips. Sew 2 white strips to either side of 1 pink strip. Press. Cut strips into 8—1 1/2" x 3 1/2" units. (Figure 3).

Figure 3

Sew 2 pink strips to either side of 1 white strip. Press. Cut strips into 4—1 1/2" x 3 1/2" units. (Figure 4).

Figure 4

Lay out the units to look like a nine-patch. Sew together. Press. (Figure 5).

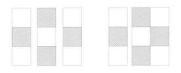

Figure 5

3. Make 4 two-color 3 1/2" squares, using (D) strips. Sew 2 purple strips to either side of 1 white strip. Press. Cut into 3 1/2" squares (Figure 6).

Figure 6

4. Make the block. Along with 5 white squares (B), lay out the block as shown in the *Block Diagram*. Pay attention to color placement so the block is stitched correctly.

5. Sew units into 5 rows. Press. Sew completed rows together to finish the block. Press all rows in the same direction.

Zip! There It Goes!

84" x 84"

Pieced by Denniele Bohannon, Harrisonville, Mo.

Quilted by Lisa Winkler, Liberty, Mo.

Montgomery Ward's last electric sewing machine

Grandma's first sewing machine was a treadle machine. I'm sure she thought it was faster than hand-sewing, but still it must have been quite a workout. By the late 1930s, Grandpa's construction company was doing well, so there was money for some of life's extras. One of those extras was an electric sewing machine for Grandma.

One day just before World War II began, Grandpa brought home a sewing machine from the *Montgomery Ward's* department store. It was reputedly the last one available in Kansas City until after the war. Whether that's true or not, Grandma must have been thrilled with this new, modern convenience.

Grandma had to get used to the power she now had. The electric machine ran much faster, so she spent some time practicing before she moved on to an actual project. "Zip! There it goes!" my dad, Donald, remembers her saying as he watched her practice.

Zip! There It Goes!
Block size: 15"

This quilt is made of 16 blocks in a straight set. Additional pieced units surround the top to extend the secondary pattern created when 4 blocks are joined together. Three plain borders frame the quilt: a plain yellow 1 1/2" inner border, a plain red 2" middle border and a plain green 4" outer border.

Fabric requirements

- Cream: 3 1/4 yards
- Dark red: 1 1/4 yard
- Medium red print: 2 1/2 yards
- Dark yellow: 3 yards
- Light yellow: 1/2 yard
- Dark green: 3 2/3 yard
- Light green: 1 yard
- Batting: queen size (90" x 108")
- Backing: 2 1/2 yards of 90" wide light-colored backing fabric or 7 1/2 yards of 42/44" wide cream fabric to match top.
- Binding: 2/3 yard for binding. This allows for 10—2" wide strips to make about 360" of binding. If you prefer 2 1/2" wide strips for binding, purchase 3/4 yard.

To get the most out of the yardage, cut the following yardage first and set aside:
From the **dark green**, cut
- 2 2/3 yards for outer border
From the **medium red**, cut
- 2 1/4 yards for the middle border
From the **dark yellow**, cut
- 2 1/4 yards for the inner border

Blocks

Cutting instructions
From cream, cut
- 96—3 7/8" squares (A)
- 64—3 1/2" squares (B)

From dark red, cut
- 64—3 7/8" squares (A)

From medium red, cut
- 16—3 1/2" squares (B)

From dark yellow, cut
- 16—3 7/8" squares (A)

From light yellow, cut
- 16—3 7/8" squares (A)

From dark green, cut
- 13—1 1/2" x full width of fabric strips (C)
- 6—1 1/2" x full width of fabric strips (D)

From light green, cut
- 11—1 1/2" x full width of fabric strips (C)
- 12—1 1/2" x full width of fabric strips (D)

Piecing the blocks

1. Referring to *How to make half-square triangle units* on page 45, make 196 half-square triangle units in 3 colorways. Use the squares (A) to make 3 1/2" half-square triangle units.

Make 128 units (Figure 1) using 64 dark red squares and 64 cream squares.

Figure 1

Make 32 units (Figure 2) using 16 dark yellow squares and 16 cream squares.

Figure 2

Make 32 units (Figure 3) using 16 light yellow squares and 16 cream squares.

Figure 3

2. Make 64 nine-patch units referring to the single block instructions. To make them, use the dark and light green strips (C).

3. Make 64 two-color 3 1/2" squares referring to the single block instructions. To make them, use the dark and light green strips (D).

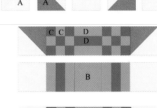

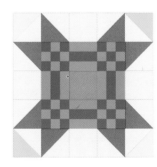

Block Assembly Diagram

Block Diagram

4. To make the 16 blocks, use the directions for piecing the single block found at the beginning of this chapter. Use the *Block Diagram* for color placement. *Note:* To alleviate bulk and ease construction of the quilt top, it is important to press the seams **open** on all blocks and additional blocks.

Additional blocks

Cutting instructions
From cream, cut
- 54—3 7/8" squares (A)
- 36—3 1/2" squares (B)
- 16—3 1/2" x 6 1/2" (C)

From dark red, cut
- 36—3 7/8" squares (A)

From dark yellow, cut
- 9—3 7/8" squares (A)

From light yellow, cut
- 9—3 7/8" squares (A)

Piecing the additional blocks

1. Referring to *How to make half-square triangle units* on page 45, make 108 half-square triangle units in 3 colorways using the squares (A). Trim units to 3 1/2". Make 72 units (Figure 1) using 36 dark red squares and 36 cream squares. Make 18 units (Figure 2) using 9 dark yellow squares and 9 cream squares. Make 18 units (Figure 3) using 9 light yellow squares and 9 cream squares.

2. Referring to the *Additional Block Diagrams* for color placement, make 16 additional blocks and 4 corner blocks in 2 colorways each. Press seams open.

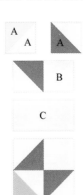

Additional Block Assembly Diagram

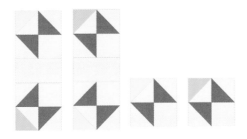

Additional Block Diagram

Borders

Inner border
Using the reserved **dark yellow**, cut
- 4—2" x 78" strips

Middle border
Using the reserved **medium red**, cut
- 4—2 1/2" x 82" strips

Outer border
Using the reserved **dark green**, cut
- 4—4 1/2" x 90" strips

Assembling the quilt top

1. Lay out a row of 4 blocks. At the beginning and end of the row, lay out the corresponding additional block, using *Quilt Top Assembly Diagram* for placement. Sew row together. Remember: **press seams open.** Repeat to make 4 rows.

Lay out top and bottom rows with corner blocks. Sew the blocks in each row together. Press seams open. Join rows together.

2. Referring to *Making mitered borders* on page 35, add the dark yellow inner borders to the sides of the quilt top. Add the inner borders to the top and bottom of quilt. Miter the corners.

3. Add the medium red middle borders to the sides of the quilt top. Add the middle borders to the top and bottom of quilt. Miter the corners.

4. Add the dark green outer borders to the sides of the quilt top. Add the outer borders to the top and bottom of quilt. Miter the corners.

Quilting and finishing the quilt

1. If using 7 1/2 yards of fabric for backing, trim selvedges. Cut into equal thirds, roughly 3 sections 90" long. Sew 3 panels together. Press.

2. Layer the top, batting and backing, making sure to center the top two layers on the backing. Baste and quilt as desired or use the suggestions below. Once quilted, bind in dark green to match the outer border.

Machine quilting suggestions. Our quilt is custom quilted quite extensively. The center of each block is filled with a 4-leaf motif. The surrounding nine-patch blocks are quilted in a 5/8" cross-hatch grid. Surrounding this, fill in the rest of the block with a meandering floral. The borders are quilted individually with a meandering leaf pattern in the inner two borders. The same floral used in the blocks is used for the outer border. Change thread color to match each fabric.

Hand quilting suggestions. Quilt in the ditch around each star within the 16 blocks and around the stars created in the surrounding the blocks. Fill in background areas with a floral motif. Use a 1" cross-hatch grid to fill in the center of the blocks. Quilt the borders with a meandering floral to match the motif used in the center of the blocks.

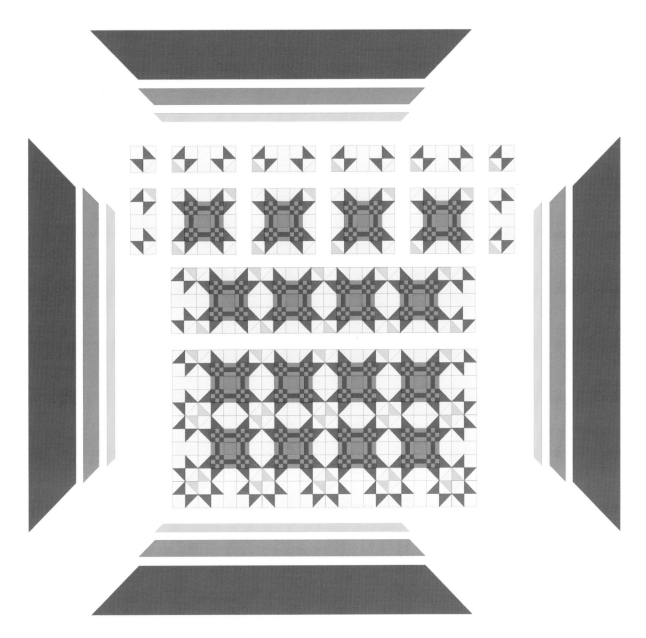

Quilt Top Assembly Diagram

Fall Star Table Runner

63" x 17"

Pieced and quilted by Jenifer Dick, Harrisonville, Mo.

Fall Star Table Runner

Block size: 15"

This table runner is made of 3 blocks and 4 partial blocks set on point.

Fabric requirements
- Black and gold print: 1/2 yard
- Gold: 1 fat quarter
- Burnt orange: 1 fat eighth
- Dark green: 1/3 yard
- Light green: 1 fat quarter
- Cream: 1 fat eighth
- Dark purple: 1 fat eighth
- Medium purple: 1 fat eighth
- Backing and binding: 2 yards black. This allows for 3—2" wide strips cut from the **length** of the fabric to make about 200" of binding. Use the remaining fabric for the backing. There is plenty of yardage if you prefer 2 1/2" wide strips.
- Batting: twin size: (72" x 90")

Blocks

Cutting instructions
From black and gold print, cut
- 16—3 7/8" squares (A)
- 20—3 1/2" squares (B)

From gold, cut
- 16—3 7/8" squares (A)

From burnt orange, cut
- 3—3 1/2" squares (E)

From dark green, cut
- 8—1 1/2" x 22" strips (C)
- 4—1 1/2" x 22" strips (D)

From light green, cut
- 7—1 1/2" x 22" strips (C)
- 2—1 1/2" x 22" strips (D)

From cream, cut
- 4—3 7/8" squares (A)

From dark purple, cut
- 2—3 7/8" squares (A)

From medium purple, cut
- 2—3 7/8" squares (A)

Piecing the blocks

1. Referring to *How to make half-square triangle units* on page 45, make 40 half-square triangle units in 3 colorways. First, make 32 half-square triangle units (Figure 1) using 16 black and 16 gold squares (A).

Figure 1   *Figure 2*   *Figure 3*

Make 4 half-square triangle units (Figure 2) using 2 cream and 2 medium purple squares (A).

Make 4 half-square triangle units (Figure 3) using 2 cream and 2 dark purple squares (A).

2. Make 16 nine-patch units referring to the single block directions. To make them, use the dark and light green strips (C).

3. Make 12 two-color 3 1/2" squares referring to the single block directions To make them, use the dark and light green strips (D).

4. To make the 3 blocks, use the directions for piecing the single block on page 24. *Note*: There are 2 colorways for the blocks. You'll make 2 blocks (Blocks A) and 1 block (Block B). Sort fabrics according to colorways and pay attention to color placement so blocks are stitched correctly.

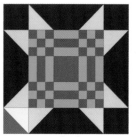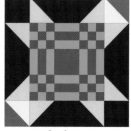

Block A   *Block B*

Partial blocks

To make the 4 additional partial blocks, use the remaining 8 black/gold half-square triangle units, 4 cream/dark purple units and 4 nine-patch units. Sort units according to the *Partial Block Diagram*. Sew together as a four-patch. Press.

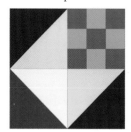

Partial Block Diagram

Assembling the quilt top

1. Lay out the blocks according to the *Quilt Top Assembly Diagram*. Pay attention to color placement so the blocks are sewn together correctly.

Quilt Top Assembly Diagram

2. Sew 1 partial block to the side of 1 block (Block A). Make sure the purples are together. Sew from the outside edge to the end of the partial block. Back stitch at the end of the seam. Press to the partial

block. Repeat with the remaining block (Block A) and another partial block.

3. Sew 2 partial blocks to either side of the remaining block (Block B) in the same manner as described above. Press.

4. Join 3 units together, making sure the purples form a quarter-square triangle unit in the center. Press.

Quilting and finishing the quilt

1. Layer the top, batting and backing, making sure to center the top two layers on the backing. Trim backing to about 4" larger on all sides. Baste and quilt as desired or use the suggestions below.

2. Once quilted, bind in black to match the outer border. To bind the 45-degree inside angles, sew from the outside edge toward the inside angle. When you get to the inside angle, position your needle down and turn the quilt top. Position the binding so it lines up properly with the edge of the quilt top and continue sewing. The outside angles are sewn as normal.

Machine quilting suggestions. Our quilt was quilted with an orange metallic thread. It was stitched in uneven, wavy rows the entire length of the runner.

Hand quilting suggestions. Quilt a different leaf motif in the center of each block. (Try tracing leaves from trees in your yard for the stencil.) For the stars created by the secondary pattern, quilt a smaller leaf motif in the center. Quilt in the ditch around the perimeter of each star.

Tip: Making mitered borders

While not every quilt requires a mitered border, for some quilts it's worth the extra effort. Miters frame the quilt in an elegant way that shows off the quiltmaker's skills. Mitered borders are not difficult but they do require forethought and planning. Here is one way to make mitered borders.

1. To determine the side border length, add the length of the quilt top plus the width of the border twice. Add a few inches to this number for a cushion. Remember to measure the quilt top through the center, not at the edge. For example, if the top is 54" long and the border is 3" wide, add 54" + 3" +3" = 60". Add a few inches for the cushion, so the border length is 63".

2. Repeat Step 1 with the quilt top width to determine the length to cut the top and bottom borders. Do this even if your quilt top is supposed to be square.

3. Fold the border in half and finger press to mark the center. Do this to the quilt top also. Line these marks up and pin the border to the quilt top starting in the center and pinning out to the corners.

4. At the corners, pin the border 1/4" in from the edge (Figure 1).When sewing on the border, start and stop at that 1/4" mark and backstitch at each end. Repeat with the adjoining border. Press toward the quilt top.

Figure 1

5. To make the miter, lay the top flat on your worktable and overlap the top border on the side border. Flip the top border underneath at a 45-degree angle so the right sides are together (Figure 2). Press on the fold.

Figure 2

6. Fold the quilt top in half diagonally. Align the borders, right sides together in a straight row (Figure 3). Pin borders together along the fold line. Sew the borders together starting exactly where the seams meet at the corner of the quilt top. Backstitch and sew to the outside edge on the fold line.

Figure 3

sew line

Open the quilt top up and flatten out the borders (Figure 4). Press. Check to see if the borders lay flat. Trim the seam allowance to 1/4". Repeat with the remaining borders.

7. If the quilt has more than one border, repeat the process, taking care to line up the miter so it flows smoothly from the center of the quilt diagonally out to the edge.

Figure 4

Chapter 3

Ducklings

The *Ducklings* block is an old block with many names. It is attractive set on point or in a straight set. In our quilt **Eggplants and Okra**, it is used in a monochromatic color scheme in two sizes. Look for the tip *How to make half-square triangle units* at the end of the chapter.

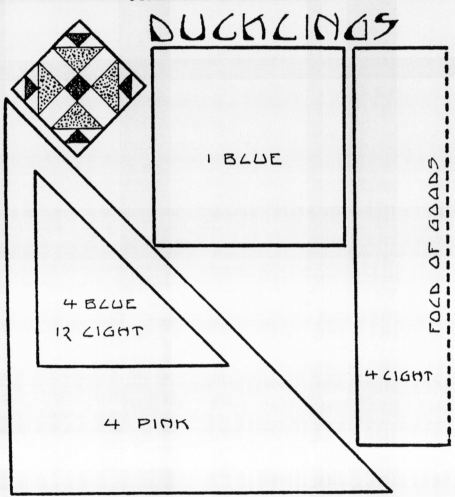

DUCKLINGS IS AN OLD PATTERN.

DUCKLINGS

1 BLUE

4 BLUE
12 LIGHT

4 PINK

FOLD OF GOODS

4 LIGHT

Ducklings block—Originally published June 11, 1932. Said <u>The Star</u>:
This rather simple block, which is thirteen inches square, may be developed in many ways, using plain or figured materials. The blocks may be alternated with plain ones of the same size. Allow for seams.

Single block instructions

Ducklings
Finished block size: 12"

This block is constructed in the nine-patch style. It is made of 4 double triangle units, 4 plain light strips and 1 plain dark square for the center. Refer to these instructions when making the quilt described in this chapter or make the single block for a sampler quilt.

Fabric requirements

- White: 1 fat quarter
- Pink print: 1 fat quarter
- Blue solid: 1 fat quarter

Cutting instructions

From white, cut
- 2—3 3/8" squares (A)
- 4—3 3/8" squares, cut in half diagonally **once** to make 8 triangles (B)
- 4—2 1/2" x 5 1/2" strips (D)

From pink, cut
- 2—5 7/8" squares, cut in half diagonally **once** to make 4 triangles (C)

From blue, cut
- 2—3 3/8" squares (A)
- 1—2 1/2" square (E)

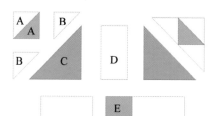

Block Assembly Diagram

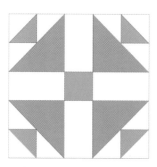

Block Assembly Diagram

Piecing the block

1. Referring to *How to make half-square triangle units* on page 45, make 4 half-square triangle units using 2 blue and 2 white squares (A). Trim units to 3".

2. Sew 2 white triangles (B) to either side of 1 half-square triangle unit (Figure 1). Press. Repeat to make 4 units.

Figure 1

3. Lay out the block as it will look once sewn as shown in the *Block Assembly Diagram*.

4. Sew 1 pink triangle (C) to 1 triangle unit (Figure 1). Press. Repeat to make 4 double triangle units.
5. Sew 2 double triangle units to either side of one white strip (D). Pay attention to color placement so the block is stitched correctly. Press. Repeat with remaining 2 double triangle units and 1 white strip (D).

6. Sew 2 white strips (D) to either side of the blue square (E). Press. Join all 3 rows together. Press.

Eggplant and Okra

50" x 50"

Pieced by Jenifer Dick, Harrisonville, Mo.

Quilted by Dana Davis, Overland Park, Kan.

The Garden

Grandma was a renaissance woman of sorts. In addition to quilting, she crocheted, knitted and sewed many clothes for herself and her children. She cooked, but she also made her own lye soap at least into the 1960s. Her list of interests amazes me. The one that probably gave her the most pleasure was her garden.

Strange and exotic things grew in that garden—at least to my way of thinking. Among these was okra, which was the strangest looking edible plant I'd ever seen. I couldn't believe someone actually thought that okra would be something good to eat!

Another plant that fascinated me was eggplant—not for its unusual name, but because of its color. I remember thinking that deep purple was the most beautiful color I had ever seen. It still ranks among my favorites.

Eggplant and Okra

Block sizes: 3", 6" and 9"

This is a medallion style quilt made of 60 blocks of various sizes: 36 plain 3" blocks, 4 plain 6" blocks, 4—9" duckling blocks and 16—6" duckling blocks. It is framed by a 4" plain border.

Fabric requirements

What makes this quilt so striking is the use of a great variety of purples. Choose shades from light lavender to dark plum to make it more interesting.

- White or pale pink: 3 yards
- Main purple: 1 1/2 yards
- Other purples:
  - Minimum: 4 fat quarters and 5-10 fat eighths
  - Maximum: 4 fat quarters and 20-30 fat eighths
- Batting: twin size (72" x 92")
- Backing: 3 yards of 42/44" wide dark purple to match top.
- Binding: 1/2 yard of the main purple. This allows for 6—2" wide strips to make about 225" of binding. If you prefer 2 1/2" wide strips for binding, purchase 2/3 yard.

To get the most out of the yardage, cut the following and set aside:

From **white**, cut
- 16" from the **width** of the fabric for borders, setting triangles, corner triangles and setting squares.

From **main purple**, cut
- 25" from the **length** of the fabric for borders, setting triangles and corner triangles.

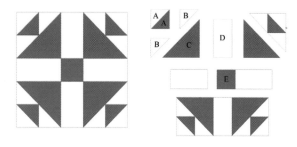

Block A   *Block A Assembly Diagram*

Blocks

Cutting instructions

Block A—9" duckling
From purple, cut
- 8—2 5/8" squares (A)
- 8—4 3/8" squares (C). Cut each square in half diagonally **once** to make 2 half-square triangles.
- 4—2 1/2" squares (E)

From white, cut
- 8—2 5/8" squares (A)
- 16—2 5/8" squares (B). Cut each square in half diagonally **once** to make 2 half-square triangles.
- 16—2 1/2" x 4" strips (D)

Block A—6" duckling
From purple, cut
- 32—2 1/8" squares (A)
- 32—3 3/8" squares (C). Cut each square in half diagonally **once** to make 2 half-square triangles.
- 16—1 1/2" squares (E)

From white, cut
- 32—2 1/8" squares (A)
- 64—2 1/8" squares (B). Cut each square in half diagonally **once** to make 2 half-square triangles.
- 64—1 1/2" x 3" strips (D)

Block B—6" plain
From purple, cut
- 8—3 3/8" squares (A)
- 4—1 1/2" square (D)

From white, cut
- 8—3 3/8" squares (A)
- 16—1 1/2" x 3" strips (C)

Block B—3" plain
From purple, cut
- 72—2 1/8" squares (A)
- 36—1" square (D)

From white, cut
- 72—2 1/8" squares (A)
- 144—1" x 1 3/4" strips (C)

Piecing the blocks

Block A—9"
1. Referring to *How to make half-square triangle units* on page 45, make 16 half-square triangle units using 8 purple and 8 white squares (A). Trim to 2 1/4".

2. To make 4 blocks, use the directions for piecing the single block found at the beginning of this chapter. Refer to the *Block A Assembly Diagram* for color placement. *Note:* To ease construction of the quilt top, press toward the white strips in the center of each block. Do this in each block that follows also.

Block A—6"
1. Referring to *How to make half-square triangle units* on page 45, make 64 half-square triangle units using 32 purple and 32 white squares (A). Trim to 1 3/4".

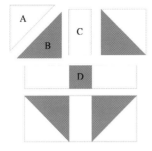

Block B   *Block B Assembly Diagram*

2. To make 16 blocks, use the directions for piecing the single block on page 38. Refer to the *Block A Assembly Diagram* for color placement.

Block B—6"

1. Referring to *How to make half-square triangle units* on page 45, make 16 half-square triangle units using 8 purple and 8 white squares (A). Trim to 3".

2. To make the 4 blocks, lay out the blocks as they will look once sewn as shown in the *Block B Diagram*. Sew blocks as a nine-patch referring to the *Block B Assembly Diagram*.

Block B—3"

1. Referring to *How to make half-square triangle units* on page 45, make 144 half-square triangle units using 72 purple and 72 white squares (A). Trim to 1 3/4".

2. To make the 36 blocks, lay out the blocks as they will look once sewn as shown in the *Block B Diagram*. Sew blocks as a nine-patch referring to the *Block B Assembly Diagram*.

Setting triangles

From the reserved **white** fabric, cut
• 6—5 1/2" squares. Cut each square in half diagonally **twice** to make 4 quarter square triangles.

From the reserved **purple** fabric, cut
• 8—5 1/2" squares. Cut each square in half diagonally **twice** to make 4 quarter square triangles.

Setting squares

From **white**, cut
• 4—3 1/2" squares
• 1—9 1/2" square

Corner triangles

From **white**, cut
• 2—3 3/8" squares. Cut each square in half diagonally **once** to make 4 half-square triangles.

From **purple**, cut
• 2—5 1/4" squares. Cut each square in half diagonally **once** to make 4 half-square triangles.

Borders

Inner border

Using the reserved **white** fabric, cut 4 strips 1" x the full width of the fabric. From these, cut 4 border strips to the following sizes:
  • 2—1" x 31 1/2"
  • 2—1" x 32 1/2"

Outer border

Using the reserved **purple** fabric, cut 4 strips 4 1/2" x the full length of the fabric. From these, cut 4 border strips to the following sizes:
  • 2—4 1/2" x 43 1/2"
  • 2—4 1/2" x 51 1/2"

Assembling the quilt top

1. Referring to the *Medallion Assembly Diagram*, lay out blocks, setting squares, setting triangles and corner triangles. Sew blocks together. Press.

Medallion Assembly Diagram

Quilt Top Assembly Diagram

2. Add the white side borders to the center medallion. Add the top and bottom borders to the medallion. Press after each border is added.

3. Referring to the *Corner Units Assembly Diagram*, lay out blocks, setting triangles and corner triangles. Sew blocks together. Press. Repeat to make 4 corner units.

Corner Units Assembly Diagram

4. Referring to the *Quilt Top Assembly Diagram*, assemble the units to complete the top. Press.

5. Add the purple side borders to the quilt top. Add the top and bottom borders to the quilt top. Press after each border is added.

Quilting and finishing the quilt

1. Trim selvedges off backing fabric. Cut into equal halves, roughly 1 1/2 yards each. Sew the panels together.

2. Layer the backing batting and top. Baste and quilt as desired or use the suggestions below. Once quilted, bind with the main purple.

Machine quilting suggestions.

This quilt lends itself to beautiful feathers or florals. Our quilt was quilted with a feathered motif in the center square. A large feathered wreath encircles the center medallion. Feathered motifs with heart centers fill in the borders. A light purple thread was chosen to stand out on the white and purple, showcasing the quilting.

Hand quilting suggestions.

This quilt can be hand quilted in the same manner as described for machine quilting. Feathered borders with an unbroken triple cable can be substituted to give it a more formal feel.

Tip: How to make half-square triangle units

There are many ways to make half-square triangle units. I use this method almost exclusively because it works every time and I don't need special tools.

The formula: add 7/8" to the desired **finished** size of the unit. This is the size to cut the fabric squares. For example, if you need a finished 2" half-square triangle unit, the formula will be: 2"+7/8"=2 7/8".

Another option is to make the units slightly bigger and then trim them to the exact size after pressing. The advantage to making the units bigger is accuracy. Unless you sew exactly on the lines with no fabric shifting, it's tricky to get the size just right. By trimming the unit down after sewing, you're guaranteed to get the correct size every time.

The disadvantage: you have an added step of trimming the squares, which takes more time. Also, you'll use more fabric, which can throw off fabric requirements.

If you do choose to make the units bigger and trim to size, increase the cut square size by 1/4" to 1/2".

To make two 2" half-square triangle units

1. Cut 2 squares, one light and one dark, 2 7/8" (finished size + 7/8"). Determine if you want to cut to size or cut over-sized for trimming later. If you choose to make over-sized units, cut the 2 squares 3 1/4".

2. Draw a line diagonally from corner to corner on the back side of the lighter fabric (figure 1).

draw line

Figure 1

3. Place the 2 squares right sides together, aligning all 4 corners. Sew 1/4" away from the drawn line on each side (figure 2).

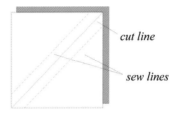

cut line

sew lines

Figure 2

4. Cut apart on the drawn line. Press toward the dark fabric. The half-square triangle unit should be 2 1/2" square. If you're trimming it, trim to the desired finished size plus seam allowance. In this case, trim to 2 1/2" (figure 3).

Figure 3

Chapter 4

Square Within Square

In this chapter, the *Square Within Square* block shows how vibrant and exciting a quilt can be. Color choice and border treatment make **Lawrence Welk is Alive and Well and Living in Syndication** an electric quilt that leaves no rest for the viewer's eye. **Dena's Doll's Quilt** gives you another option: using this challenging quilt block as a single block quilt. Look for a tip—*Making pieced borders work*—at the end of the chapter.

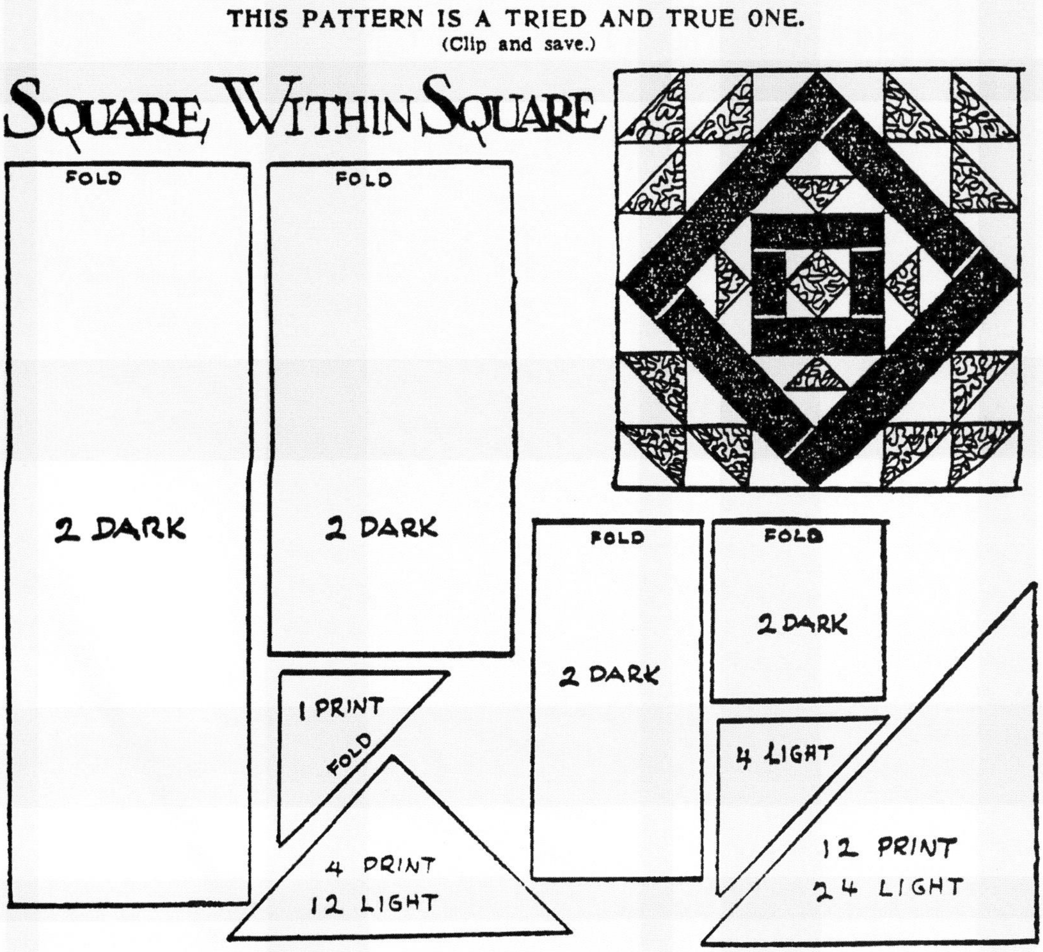

THIS PATTERN IS A TRIED AND TRUE ONE.
(Clip and save.)

SQUARE WITHIN SQUARE

FOLD — FOLD

2 DARK — 2 DARK

FOLD — FOLD

2 DARK — 2 DARK

1 PRINT
FOLD

4 PRINT
12 LIGHT

4 LIGHT

12 PRINT
24 LIGHT

Square Within Square block—Originally published May 17, 1933. Said The Star:
The square within the square is an old pattern that tests the skill of the quilt maker.
The squares should be of the same material.

Single block instructions

Square Within Square
Finished block size: 12"

This block is comprised of 65 pieces in 3 colors— white, a dark solid and a print. Refer back to these instructions when making the two quilts described in this chapter or make the single block for a sampler quilt.

Fabric requirements

- Green solid: 1 fat quarter
- Green print: 1 fat eighth
- White: 1 fat quarter

Cutting instructions
From white, cut
- 6—2 7/8" squares (A)
- 6—2 7/8" squares, cut in half diagonally to make 12 triangles (B)
- 2—2 1/4" squares (E)
- 4—2 1/4" squares, cut in half diagonally to make 8 triangles (F)
- 2—1 7/8" squares, cut in half diagonally to make 4 triangles (I)

From green solid, cut
- 2—1 7/8" x 6 1/2" strips (C)
- 2—1 7/8" x 9" strips (D)
- 2—1 1/2" x 2 1/2" strips (G)
- 2—1 1/2" x 4 1/2" strips (H)
From green print, cut
- 6—2 7/8" squares (A)
- 2—2 1/4" squares (E)
- 1—1 7/8" square (J)

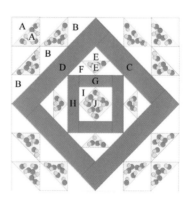

Block Diagram

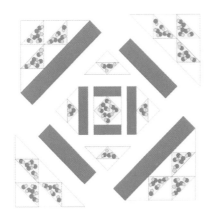

Block Assembly Diagram

Piecing the block

1. Make 1—2 1/2" square within a square unit for the center. You'll need 1 green print square (J) and 4 white triangles (I). Sew 4 triangles around the square. To make this unit, refer to The *No pin method for making the"square within a square unit* on page 77.

2. Sew short green solid strips (G) to the sides of the square within a square unit. Press. Sew long green solid strips (H) to the opposite sides of unit. Press.

3. Make 4 triangle units to surround the center unit. Using 2 white squares (E) and 2 green print squares (E), make 4—1 7/8" half-square triangle units. Refer to *How to make half-square triangle units* on page 45 for instructions. Next, sew 2 triangles (F) to adjoining sides of 1 half-square triangle unit (Figure 1). Press away from half-square triangle unit. Repeat to make 4 units. Sew around the block. Press.

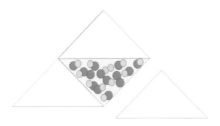

Figure 1

4. Sew the short green solid strips (C) to the sides of the block. Press. Sew the long green solid strips (D) to the opposite sides. Press.

5. Make 4 triangle units to finish the block (Figure 2). Using 6 white squares (A) and 6 green print squares (A), make 12—2 1/2" half-square triangle units.

Next, using 3 white triangles (B), lay out the unit. Sew together as shown, pressing after each seam is sewn. Repeat to make 4 units. Sew these to the block. Press.

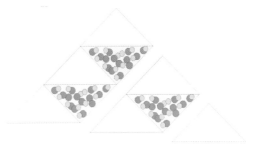

Figure 2

Lawrence Welk is Alive and Well and Living in Syndication

96" x 96"

Pieced by Jenifer Dick, Harrisonville, Mo.

Quilted by Dana Davis, Overland Park, Kan.

Isn't Lawrence Welk still entertaining viewers today?

Grandma liked wholesome television. If you called her during *The Waltons*, she would ask you to call back later. One program in particular I remember her watching was *The Lawrence Welk Show*. It seemed as though it was always on in her living room. I assume it was in syndication even then (in the mid-'70s) because I can remember thinking the hairstyles were so crazy-looking on the women singers.

I don't have a memory of Grandma actually sitting down to watch the program. She had it on while she did her daily chores. Occasionally she would run in from another room to watch a favorite singer or to hear a favorite song. When I was young, I thought Lawrence Welk was on 24 hours a day.

Lawrence Welk is Alive and Well and Living in Syndication

Block size: 18"

This quilt is made of 16 Square Within Square blocks set side by side. Three borders frame the quilt—a 1 1/2" plain inner border, a 4 1/4" pieced middle border, and a 6" pieced outer border.

Fabric requirements
- Black: 6 yards
- Tan: 5 yards
- Red: 4 1/3 yards
- Binding: 2/3 yards to match top. This will provide for 10 to 11—2" wide strips to make about 400" of binding. If you prefer 2 1/2" wide binding, purchase 7/8 yard.
- Batting: king size (120" x 120")

- Backing: 3 yards 108" wide backing fabric or 8 1/2 yards of 42/44" wide fabric to match top.

Special tools
- Template plastic for making the pieced outer border.
- Spray starch

To get the most from the yardage, cut the following and set aside.

From **black**, cut
- 2 1/3 yards for pieced middle border
- 1 1/4 yards for pieced outer border

From **tan**, cut
- 1 1/4 yards for pieced outer border

From **red**, cut
- 2 1/3 yards for both plain inner and pieced middle border

Blocks

Cutting instructions
From black, cut
- 32—3 7/8" squares (A)
- 32—2" x 3 1/2" strips (G)
- 32—2" x 6 1/2" strips (H)
- 32—2 5/8" x 9" strips (C)
- 32—2 5/8" x 13 1/4" strips (D)

From tan, cut
- 96—3 7/8" squares (A)
- 96—3 7/8" squares, cut in half diagonally to make 12 triangles (B)
- 32—3" squares (E)
- 64—3" squares, cut in half diagonally to make 8 triangles (F)
- 32—2 3/8" squares, cut in half diagonally to make 4 triangles (I)

From red, cut
- 64—3 7/8" squares (A)

- 32—3" squares (E)
- 16—2 3/8" square (J)

Piecing the blocks

1. Make 64—2 5/8" half-square triangle units using 32 red and 32 tan squares (E).

2. Make 64—3 1/2" half-square triangle units using 32 black and 32 tan squares (A).

3. Make 128—3 1/2" half-square triangle units using 64 red and 64 tan squares (A).

4. Sort the fabrics into 16 blocks, using the *Color Placement Guide* to make sure all fabrics are in the correct order. To make the 16 blocks, use the directions for piecing the single block found at the beginning of this chapter.

Color Placement Guide

Borders

Inner border
Because this quilt has pieced borders, the exact measurement of this inner border is crucial for the success of the quilt. Using the reserved red fabric, cut off about 10" lengthwise along the selvedge. Reserve this until you have made the pieced middle and outer

borders. Then, refer to *Making pieced borders work* on page 61 to determine the exact measurements for your quilt top.

The approximate size of the inner borders will be:
- 2—2" x 72 1/2" strips
- 2—2" x 75 1/2" strips

Middle pieced border

From the reserved red, cut
- 17—5 1/2" squares. Cut each square in half diagonally twice to make 68 quarter-square triangles.
- 2—3 1/8" squares, cut in half diagonally once to make 4 half-square triangles.

From the reserved black, cut
- 72—3 5/8" squares
- 17—5 1/2" squares, cut in half diagonally twice to make 68 quarter-square triangles.
- 6—3 1/8" squares, cut in half diagonally once to make 12 half-square triangles.

Note: Each side border has 17 black squares, 16 black and 16 red quarter-square triangles, 2 black and 2 red half-square triangles. The top and bottom borders have 19 black squares, 17 black and 17 red quarter-square triangles and 4 black half-square triangles.

Piecing the middle border

1. To make 1 side border, sew a red quarter-square triangle to the side of a black square. Press. Sew a black quarter-square triangle to the opposite side of the black square. Press. Make 15 of these units. Sew units together in a long strip. Press. (Figure 1)

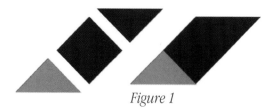

Figure 1

Next, make 2 end units. For the first, sew a black quarter-square triangle to the side of a black square. Press. Sew 1 red half-square triangle to the opposite side. Sew 1 black half-square triangle to the adjoining side. (Figure 2)

Figure 2

For the second end unit, sew a red quarter-square triangle to the side of a black square. Press. Sew 1 black half-square triangle to the opposite side. Sew 1 red half-square triangle to the adjoining side. (Figure 3)

Figure 3

Sew units to the ends of the pieced strip. Press. Repeat to make another side border.

2. To make top border, make 17 of the *Figure 1* units as described above. Next, make 2 end units. Sew a black quarter-square triangle to the side of a black square. Press. Sew 2 black half-square triangles to the opposite sides. Press. (Figure 4)

Figure 4

To make the second end unit, sew a red quarter-square triangle to the side of a black square. Press. Sew 2 black half-square triangles to the opposite sides. Press. (Figure 5).

Figure 5

Sew end units to the ends of the pieced strip. Press. Repeat to make the bottom border.

You should now have 4 pieced middle borders that measure:
- 2—4 3/4" x 75 1/2"
- 2—4 3/4" x 84"

Outer pieced border
Note: To prevent the bias edges of the triangles from stretching, use a generous amount of spray starch on the black and tan fabrics before cutting.

Making the templates

Trace templates A and B onto template plastic. Make sure to include the seam allowance and to draw the grain line arrow on the plastic.

Cut out the shapes on the solid line, being careful to make the edges smooth and accurate. Label the pieces A and B on the front side.

From the reserved black, cut
- 6—6 1/2" x the full width of fabric strips. These will be cut into triangles later.
- 4—6 1/2" squares

From the reserved tan, cut
- 6—6 1/2" x the full width of fabric strips. These will be cut into triangles later.

Note: Each border has 14 tan triangles, 13 black triangles and 2 black half-triangles. Two borders will have black corner squares on each end.

Piecing the outer border

1. Cut 52 black triangles, using template A. Layer up to 4 strips of black fabric. Place the base of A along the bottom edge of the strip. Use a rotary cutter to cut along both sides, being careful not to cut into the template. (Figure 6). To avoid waste, invert A and line up the base on the opposite side of the strip and the edge of the previously cut triangle. Continue cutting along the strip.

Figure 6

2. Cut 8 half-triangles. Using leftover black fabric from the strips used above, stack 2 layers of fabric **right sides together**. Place the base of template B along the edge of the strip. Cut along both sides (Figure 7). To avoid waste, invert B to line up the base on the opposite side of the strip and the edge of the previously cut triangle. Continue cutting along the strip.

Figure 7

3. Cut 56 tan triangles in the same way as described above in step 1.

4. To make 1 side border, sew a black triangle to a tan triangle. (Figure 8). Be sure to offset the edges by 1/4" to ensure they line up correctly after they are sewn. Make 13 of these units.

Figure 8

Sew the units together in a long strip. Press. Sew 1 half-triangle to the end of the strip. (Figure 9)

Figure 9

Next, make 1 end unit. Sew 1 half-triangle to 1 tan triangle. (Figure 10) Press. Sew to the end of strip. Press.

Figure 10

Repeat the above steps to make the 3 remaining borders. On 2 of the borders, add the black 6 1/2" corner squares to each end. Press.

You should now have 4 pieced borders that measure:
- 2—6 1/2" x 84"
- 2—6 1/2" x 96 1/2"

Assembling the quilt top

1. Referring to the *Quilt Top Assembly Diagram*, lay out the blocks in 4 rows of 4 blocks each. Sew together in rows. Press. Stitch the rows together. Press.

2. Add the short red inner borders to the sides of the quilt top. Add the long inner borders to the top and bottom of quilt. *Note:* Press after each border is added.

3. Add the short middle borders to the sides of the quilt top. Add the long middle borders to the top and bottom of quilt.

4. Add the short outer borders to the sides of the quilt top. Add the long outer borders to the top and bottom of quilt.

Quilting and finishing the quilt

1. If you use 8 1/2 yards of 42/44" wide fabric for the backing, trim off the selvedges. Cut this yardage into equal thirds, roughly 3 sections 100" long. Sew the panels together and press.

2. Layer the backing, batting and top. Baste and quilt as desired or follow the quilting suggestions below. Once quilted, bind with a fabric that matches the top.

Machine quilting suggestions. Our quilt was quilted using tan thread to match the fabric in the top. The pattern is a loose, over-all pantograph. It has spiky points to accentuate the numerous points in the top. You could easily use a loopy, flowery all-over design to contrast and soften all the angles. Custom quilting would also highlight the blocks and emphasize the borders.

Hand quilting suggestions. For the ambitious hand quilter, choose an 18" pattern to fill each block. An angular geometric pattern would complement the graphic nature of the block. Echo-quilt about 1/2" apart around the triangles in the border twice. Use thread that matches the fabric.

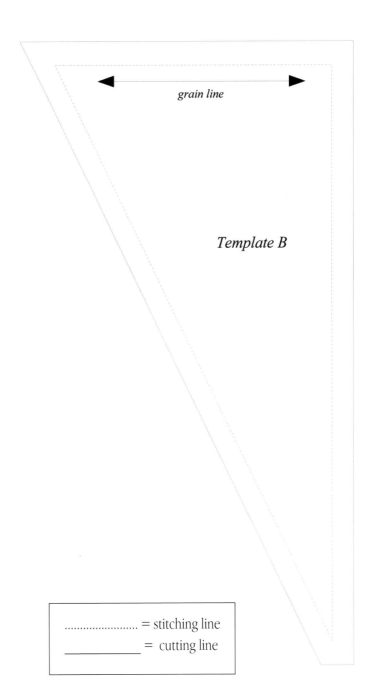

grain line

Template B

.... = stitching line

_____ = cutting line

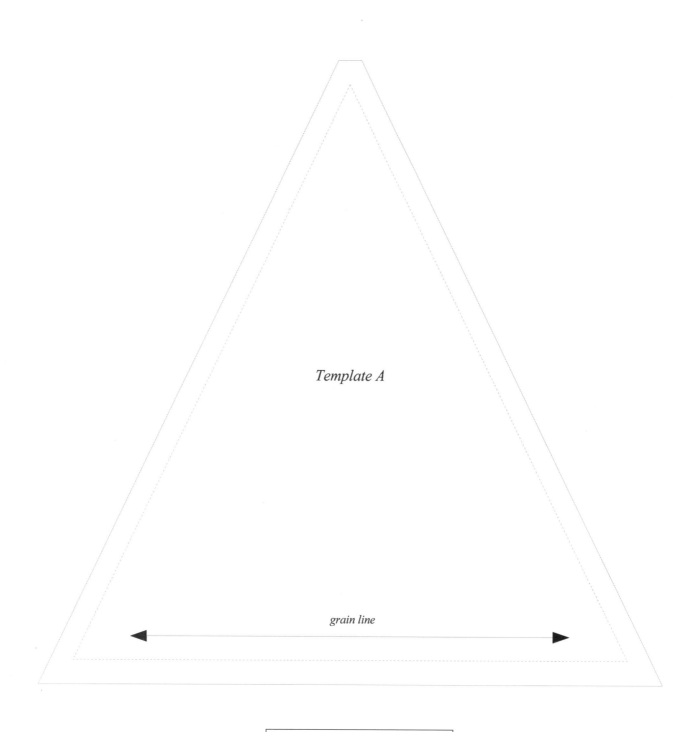

Template A

grain line

.... = stitching line

_____ = cutting line

Quilt Top Assembly Diagram

Dena's Doll's Quilt

18 1/4" x 18 1/4"

Pieced by Jenifer Dick, Harrisonville, Mo.

Quilted by Mildred Randall, Harrisonville, Mo.

Dena's Doll's Quilt

This quilt is made of one Square Within Square block with no borders.

Fabric requirements

- Pink stripe: 1/2 yard—includes binding
- Yellow: 1 fat quarter
- Hot pink: 1 fat quarter
- Lime green: 1 fat eighth
- Backing: piece together left-over fabrics from the top to make a 20" square OR purchase 2/3 yard to match top.
- Batting: batting (36" x 45")

Cutting instructions

From pink stripe, cut
- 2—2" x 3 1/2"strips (G)
- 2—2" x 6 1/2" strips (H)
- 2—2 5/8" x 9" strips (C)
- 2—2 5/8" x 13 1/4" strips (D)
- 6 strips—2" x 18" for binding. This makes about 100" of binding. If you prefer 2 1/2" wide strips for binding, cut 6 strips—2 1/2" x 18".

From yellow, cut
- 6—3 7/8" squares (A)
- 6—3 7/8" squares, cut in half diagonally to make 12 triangles (B)
- 2—3" squares (E)
- 4—3" squares, cut in half diagonally to make 8 triangles (F)
- 2—2 3/8" squares, cut in half diagonally to make 4 triangles (I)

From hot pink, cut
- 4—3 7/8" squares (A)
- 1—2 3/8" square (J)

From lime green, cut
- 2—3 7/8" squares (A)
- 2—3" squares (E)

Piecing the quilt

1. Referring to *How to make half-square triangle units* on page 45, make 4—2 5/8" half-square triangle units using 2 yellow and 2 lime squares (E).

2. Make 8—3 1/2" half-square triangle units using 4 hot pink and 4 yellow squares (A).

3. Make 4—3 1/2" half-square triangle units using 4 lime and 4 yellow squares (A).

4. Sort fabrics according to the *Color Placement Guide*. Make 1 block using the directions for piecing the single block on page 48.

Color Placement Guide

Quilting and finishing the quilt

1. Layer the backing, batting and top. Baste and quilt as desired or use the suggestions below. Once quilted, bind in the pink stripe fabric.

Machine quilting suggestions.
Because of its size, this is a perfect quilt for practicing free motion quilting skills on your regular sewing machine. An all-over stipple or other pattern with a children's theme would be appropriate, or use the walking foot to stitch 1/4" around each yellow shape.

Hand quilting suggestions.
Quilt 1/4" around each yellow shape, using thread to match the background fabric. This traditional technique emphasizes the colored shapes and makes them appear to "pop" out of the quilt.

Tip: Making pieced borders work

Pieced borders are a beautiful addition to many quilts, but they can present challenges. Because it's more difficult to fit the border to the quilt top, they tend to be either slightly too long or too short. Trying to fit one of these borders on can cause ripples along the edges of the quilt.

Inserting plain borders can provide a simple solution. The trick is figuring out the border size that will bridge the distance between the quilt top and the pieced borders. To do this, use the following formula:

1. Measure the length of the quilt top. Be sure to measure through the center of the top, not at the edge.

2. Measure the length of the pieced side border.

3. Subtract the quilt top measurement from the pieced border measurement. Divide this number by 2. This is the width of the inner border.

For example, if the quilt top is 75" wide and the pieced border measures 80", subtract 75 from 80:
80" - 75" = 5"
Then, divide this number by 2:
5" - 2 = 2 1/2"

The inner side border width is 2 1/2". To this number, **add 1/2" for seam allowances.**

4. The length of the inner side border is the same as the width of the quilt top. In the example above, the length is 75". Do not add a seam allowance to this number.

Cut 2 side borders 3" x 75".

5. Sew the inner side borders to the quilt top. Press. Now, measure the width of the quilt top through the center, including the two borders. This should be the length of the top and bottom inner borders. In the example above, the width of the top, with side borders added, is 80", which should be the same as the length of the pieced border. If it is not, refigure the math, making sure you added the seam allowance in step 3.

Cut 2 top and bottom borders, 3" x 80".

Modified formula for plain borders

This formula works for adding pieced borders to a quilt top, but even if your quilt has only plain borders, it's wise to use a modified version of the formula to keep the borders straight and ripple-free.

Most quilt patterns give exact measurements to cut the borders for the top. Because everyone pieces a little differently, these numbers don't always match what you've actually sewn. By using the following formula, you can determine the length to cut the borders to fit your individual quilt top.

1. Measure the length of the quilt top. Be sure to measure through the center of the top, not at the edge. This is the length to cut the side borders. The width remains the same as given in the pattern.

2. Sew these borders to the quilt top. Press. Measure the width through the center of the top, including the side borders. This is the length to cut the top and bottom borders.

3. Remember to measure both the length and width of the quilt top. Even a square quilt top can be off by 1/2" to 1".

Chapter 5

Squirrel in a Cage

The same block can yield dramatically different quilts—all because of color choices. We use the classic *Squirrel in a Cage* block in this chapter to make both the elegant and intricate-looking **Black Walnut Cake and Gooseberry Pie** quilt and the very casual **Debra's Picnic Quilt**. Look for a tip—the *No-pin method for making the Square Within Square unit*—at the end of the chapter.

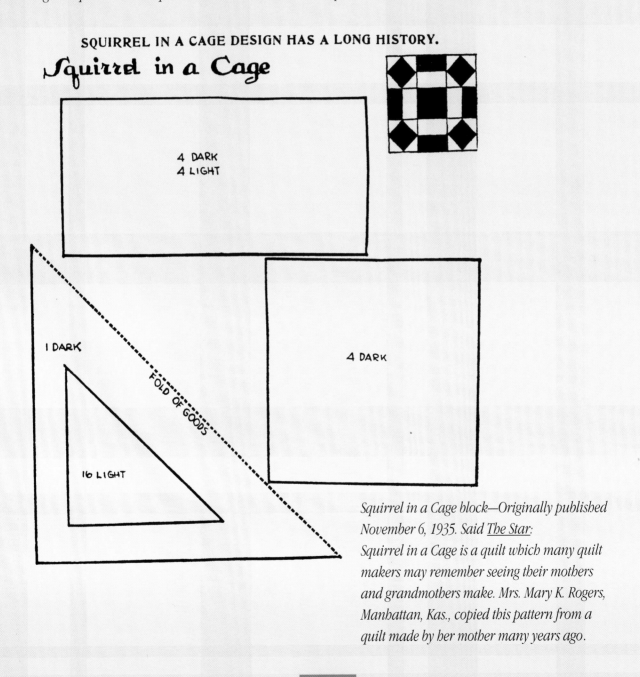

SQUIRREL IN A CAGE DESIGN HAS A LONG HISTORY.

Squirrel in a Cage

4 DARK
4 LIGHT

1 DARK

FOLD OF GOODS

16 LIGHT

4 DARK

Squirrel in a Cage block—Originally published November 6, 1935. Said <u>The Star</u>:
Squirrel in a Cage is a quilt which many quilt makers may remember seeing their mothers and grandmothers make. Mrs. Mary K. Rogers, Manhattan, Kas., copied this pattern from a quilt made by her mother many years ago.

Single block instructions

Squirrel in a Cage
Finished block size: 12"

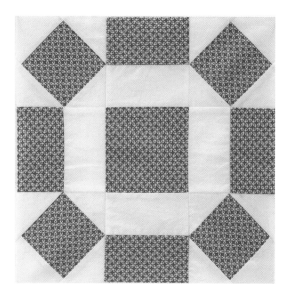

This block is constructed as a simple nine-patch. It is made of four "square within a square" units, four two-color square units and one solid square. Refer to these instructions when making the two quilts described in this chapter, or make the single block for a sampler quilt.

Fabric requirements

- Red: 1 fat quarter
- White: 1 fat quarter

Cutting instructions

From white, cut
- 8—2 7/8" squares, cut in half diagonally to make 16 triangles (A)
- 4—4 1/2" x 2 1/2" strips (C)

From red, cut
- 4—3 3/8" squares (B)
- 4—4 1/2" x 2 1/2" strips (C)
- 1—4 1/2" square (D)

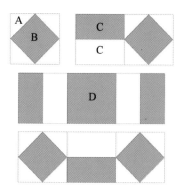

Block Assembly Diagram

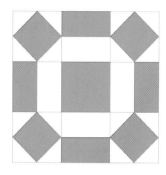

Block Diagram

Piecing the block

1. Make 4—4 1/2" "square within a square" units for the 4 outer corners. You'll need 4 red 3 3/8" squares (B) and 16 white triangles (A). Sew 4 triangles around the square. To make these units, refer to *The No-pin method for making the square within a square unit* on page 77.

2. Make 4 two-color 4 1/2" squares. Sew 1 red rectangle (C) to 1 white rectangle (C). Press to red. Repeat to make 4 units.

3. Make the block. Along with the 1 red square (D), lay out the block as it will look once sewn as shown in *Block Assembly Diagram*. Pay attention to color placement so the block is stitched correctly.

4. Sew together as you would sew a simple nine-patch block. First, sew units into 3 rows. Press. Sew completed rows together to complete the block. Press.

Black Walnut Cake and Gooseberry Pie

92" x 92"

Pieced by Jenifer Dick, Harrisonville, Mo.

Quilted by Sherri Dolly, Overland Park, Kan.

The Black Walnut Cake Incident

We never got plain chocolate cake for our birthday. Grandma always had, in my way of thinking, odd confections at her house. My ninth birthday was no different. I was so excited to have cake when we got to her house. To my dismay, there was a big beautiful black walnut cake waiting for me. When I was young, I had an unfortunate reaction to black walnuts. Just the smell of them sent me running to the bathroom. Needless to say, I was horrified by the sight of that cake. Grandma, of course, felt terrible. In an attempt to make me happier, she brought out a gooseberry pie she had on hand. But gooseberries were probably second on my dislike list as a child. Poor Grandma! I don't remember one present I got that year, but the Black Walnut Cake Incident is still laughed about today in my family!

Black Walnut Cake and Gooseberry Pie

Block size: 12"

This quilt is made of 25 blocks set on point. The blocks are separated by 1" cream sashing with black cornerstones. Three borders frame the quilt: a plain black 2" inner border; a green and cream 3" pieced border; and a plain black 4" outer border.

Fabric requirements
- Black: 5 1/2 yards
- Lime green: 2 yards
- Cream: 4 yards
- Batting: king size (120" x 120")
- Backing: 108" wide light-colored backing fabric or 8 1/2 yards of 42/44" wide cream fabric to match top.
- Binding: 2/3 yard black. This allows for 10 to 11—2" wide strips to make about 400" of binding. If you prefer 2 1/2" wide strips for binding, purchase 3/4 yard.

To get the most out of the yardage, cut the following from the **black** fabric first and set aside:
- 3 1/4 yards for borders, setting triangles and corner triangles.

Blocks

Cutting instructions
From black, cut
- 12 strips—2 1/2" x the full width of fabric (C)
- 16—4 1/2" squares (D)
- 72—2 7/8" squares, cut in half diagonally to make 144 triangles (A)
From cream, cut
- 12 strips 2 1/2" x the full width of fabric (C)
- 128—2 7/8" squares, cut in half diagonally to make 256 triangles (A)
From green, cut
- 100—3 3/8" squares (B)
- 9—4 1/2" squares (D)

Piecing the blocks

1. Make strip sets by sewing one 2 1/2" cream strip to one 2 1/2" black strip. Press to the dark and cut into 4 1/2" squares. Repeat with remaining strips to make 100—4 1/2" squares.

2. To make the 25 blocks, use the directions for piecing the single block found at the beginning of this chapter. *Note:* There are 2 colorways for the blocks. Make 16 with black centers (Block A) and 9 with green centers (Block B). Sort fabrics according to colorways and pay attention to color placement so blocks are stitched correctly.

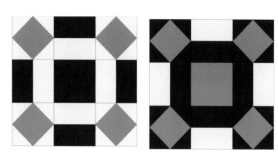

Block A   *Block B*

Sashing

Cutting instructions
From black, cut
• 40—1 1/2" squares

From cream, cut
• 22-23 strips—1 1/2" x the full width of fabric. Cut into 64—1 1/2" x 12 1/2" strips.

Borders

Inner border
Because this quilt has pieced borders, the exact measurement of this inner border is crucial for the success of the quilt. Using the reserved black fabric, cut off about 10" lengthwise along the selvedge. Reserve this until you have made the pieced middle and outer borders. Then, refer to *Making pieced borders work* on page 61 to determine the exact measurements for your quilt top.

Using the reserved 3 1/4 yards black fabric, cut:
• 2 strips—75 1/2" x 2"
• 2 strips—78 1/2" x 2"

Outer border
Using the reserved 3 1/4 yards black fabric, cut:
• 2 strips—84 1/2" x 4 1/2"
• 2 strips—92 1/2" x 4 1/2"

Pieced diamond border

Cutting instructions
From green, cut
• 104—2 5/8" squares
• 4—3 1/2" squares

From cream, cut
• 50—4 1/4" squares. Cut each square in half diagonally **twice** to make 200 quarter-square triangles.
• 8—2 3/4" squares. Cut each square in half diagonally **once** to make 16 half-square triangles.

Note: Each side border has 26 green squares, 50 cream quarter-square triangles and 4 cream half-square triangles. Two borders will have green corner squares on each end.

Piecing the diamond border

1. To make a pieced border, sew 2 cream quarter-square triangles to either side of 1 green square (Figure 1). Press. Make 24 of these units. Sew units together in a long strip. Press. Next, make 2 end units. Sew 1 quarter-square triangle to 1 side of a green square. Press. Sew 2 half-square triangles to the opposite 2 sides (Figure 2). Repeat with another green square and triangles.

Sew units to the ends of the pieced strip. Press. Repeat to make 3 remaining borders.

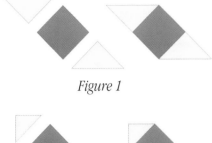

Figure 1

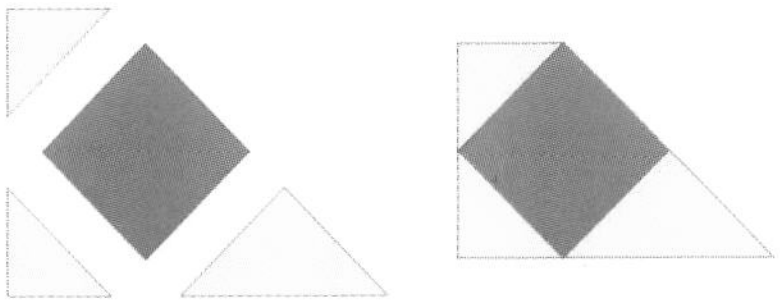

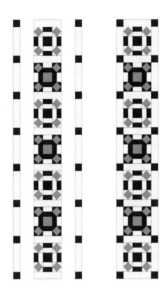

Figure 2

2. On 2 of the borders, add a green 3 1/2" corner square to each end. Press.

You should have 4 pieced borders in approximately the following sizes:
• 2 strips—78 1/2" x 3 1/2"
• 2 strips—84 1/2" x 3 1/2"

Setting triangles

1. From the remaining 3 1/4 yards of black fabric, cut 3—21" squares.
2. Cut each square in half diagonally **twice** to make 12 setting triangles.

Corner triangles

1. From remaining black fabric, cut 2—10 3/4" squares.

2. Cut each square in half diagonally **once** to make 4 corner triangles.

Assembling the quilt top

1. Make block strip units and sashing units. Sew 8 sashing strips to 7 blocks, paying attention to block placement. Press to sashing. Next, sew 8 cornerstones to 7 sashing strips. Press to sashing. Repeat to make a second sashing unit.

Sew sashing units to either side of the block strip unit. Press. (Figure 3)

Figure 3

2. Repeat this process, sewing 5 blocks together with 6 sashing strips, paying attention to block placement. Press. Sew 6 cornerstones to 5 sashing strips. Press. Sew sashing unit to block strip unit. To finish, sew a setting triangle to each end (Figure 4). Press. Make 2 of these units.

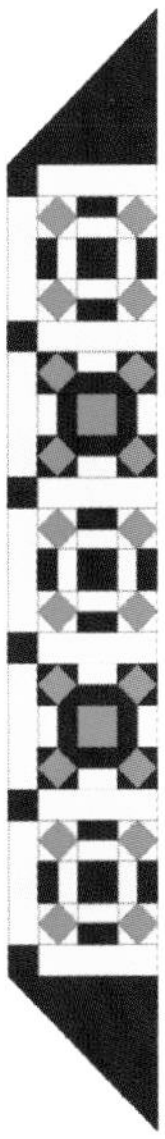

Figure 4

3. Repeat with remaining blocks, to make 2 units of 3 blocks (Figure 5) and 2 units of 1 block (Figure 6).

Figure 5

Figure 6

4. Lay out these units according to the *Quilt Top Assembly Diagram*. Join rows together. Add corner triangles to the 4 corners. Press.

5. Add the short black inner borders to the sides of the quilt top. Add the long inner borders to the top and bottom of quilt. *Note:* Press after each border is added.

6. Add the short pieced borders to the sides of the quilt top. Add the long pieced borders to the top and bottom of quilt.

7. Add the short black outer borders to the sides of the quilt top. Add the long black outer borders to the top and bottom of quilt.

Quilting and finishing the quilt

1. If using 8 1/2 yards of fabric for backing, trim selvedges. Cut into equal thirds, roughly 3 sections 100" long. Sew 3 panels together and press.

2. Layer the top, batting and backing, making sure to center the top two layers on the backing. Trim backing to about 4" larger on all sides. Baste and quilt as desired or use the suggestions below. Once quilted, bind in black to match the outer border.

Machine quilting suggestions. This quilt is very graphic, so the quilting can be secondary to the design. An all-over pattern, pantograph would be appropriate. Choose a geometric pattern to accent the angles in the quilt or a curving, flowing pattern to soften the angles. Your long-arm quilter may offer more suggestions.

This quilt is custom quilted quite extensively. Each block is filled with a leaf and vine wreath to match the leaf print in the green fabric. A long vining leaf meander fills in the sashing areas. The outer border is stitched in straight rows about 1" apart from the quilt center to the outside edge.

Hand quilting suggestions. Stitch an outline 1/4" around each shape within the blocks and sashing. Use fancier quilting such as a feather design in the shape of a triangle to fill in the setting triangles. A border treatment as described above or a crosshatch in the same size as the pieced border diamonds create a frame for the quilt.

Quilt Top Assembly Diagram

Debra's Picnic Quilt

68" x 68"

Pieced by Debra J. Fieth, Lee's Summit, Mo.

Quilted by Lisa Winkler, Liberty, Mo.

Debra's Picnic Quilt

Block size: 18"

This quilt is made of 9 blocks in a straight set. There is no sashing. Three plain borders frame the quilt: a cream 1" inner border; a red 2" middle border; and a blue 4" outer border.

Fabric requirements

- Blue: 2 yards
- Red: 1 2/3 yards
- Cream: choose two colors of cream that have some noticeable contrast, but blend together well.
  - Cream #1: 1 1/4 yards
  - Cream #2: 1 1/4 yards
- Batting: twin size (72" x 90")
- Backing: 4 1/4 yards of 42/44" wide dark fabric to match top
- Binding: 1/2 yard of either blue to match outer border or red to accent middle border. This allows for 15—2" wide strips to make about 300" of binding. If you prefer 2 1/2" wide strips for binding, purchase 2/3 yard.

Blocks

Cutting instructions

From blue, cut

- 4 strips—4 1/2" x the full length of fabric for outer border. These will be cut to size later.
- 9—6 1/2" squares (E)

From red, cut

- 5 strips—2 1/2" x the full length of fabric for middle border. These will be pieced to size later.
- 72—3 7/8" squares (A)
- 36—3 1/2" x 6 1/2" rectangles (D)

From cream #1, cut

- 5 strips—1 1/2" x the full length of fabric for inner border. These will be pieced to size later.
- 36—3 7/8" squares (C)
- 16—3 1/2" x 6 1/2" rectangles (D)

From cream #2, cut

- 36—3 7/8" squares (B)
- 20—3 1/2" x 6 1/2" rectangles (D)

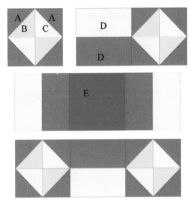

Block Assembly Diagram

Piecing the blocks

1. Referring to *How to make half-square triangle units* on page 45, make 144 half-square triangles in 2 colorways. First, make 72 half-square triangles (Figure 1) using 36 red squares (A) and 36 cream #1 squares (C). Next, repeat to make another 72 half-square triangles (Figure 2) using 36 red squares (A) and 36 cream #2 squares (B).

Figure 1   *Figure 2*

2. Make 36 square within a square units (Figure 3). Lay out 2 red/cream #1 half-square

triangles and two red/cream #2 half-square triangles (Figure 4). Pay attention to color placement so blocks are stitched correctly. Sew together as you would a simple four-patch block. Repeat with remaining half-square triangles to make 36 units.

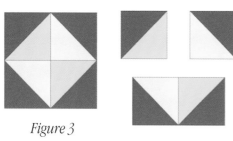

Figure 3

Figure 4

3. Make 36 two-color 6 1/2" squares in 2 colorways. First, stitch 16 red rectangles (D) to 16 cream #1 rectangles (D) along the 6 1/2" sides. Press to the red. (Figure 5). Repeat with 20 red rectangles and 20 cream #2 rectangles (Figure 6).

Figure 5   *Figure 6*

4. To make the 9 blocks, use the directions for piecing the single block on page 64. *Note:* There are 2 colorways for the blocks. You'll make 4 blocks using the Figure 5 unit (Block A) and 5 blocks using the Figure 6 unit (Block B). Sort fabrics according to colorways and pay attention to color placement so blocks are stitched correctly.

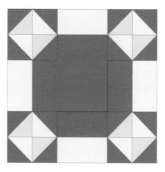

Block A

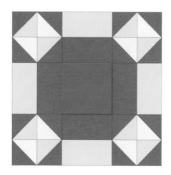

Block B

Borders

Inner border

Using the cream #1 strips cut earlier, piece 4 border strips and cut to the following sizes:
- 2 strips—1 1/2" x 54 1/2"
- 2 strip—1 1/2" x 56 1/2"

Middle border

Using the red strips cut earlier, piece 4 border strips and cut to the following sizes:
- 2 strips—2 1/2" x 56 1/2"
- 2 strips—2 1/2" x 60 1/2"

Outer border

Using the blue strips cut earlier, cut:
- 2 strips—4 1/2" x 60 1/2"
- 2 strips—4 1/2" x 68 1/2"

Assembling the quilt top

1. Join the 9 blocks together as you would sew a nine-patch block,. making sure to alternate the two colorways as shown in the *Quilt Top Assembly Diagram*.

2. Add the short, cream inner borders to the sides of the quilt top. Add the long, cream inner borders to the top and bottom of quilt. *Note:* Press after each border is added.

3. Add the short, red middle borders to the sides of the quilt top. Add the long, red pieced borders to the top and bottom of quilt.

4. Add the short, blue outer borders to the sides of the quilt top. Add the long, blue outer borders to the top and bottom of quilt.

Quilting and finishing the quilt

Trim selvedges off the backing fabric and cut into 2 equal pieces about 2 1/8 yards each. Sew panels together and press.

Layer the backing, batting and top. Baste and quilt as desired or use the suggestions below. Once quilted, bind in the color of your choice.

Machine-quilting suggestions. If you intend to use this quilt as a picnic quilt, you'll want it to be durable and strong. Close machine quilting with an all-over pattern will create a quilt that can withstand outside use and be machine washable.

The example shown is custom quilted extensively. Each blue center square has a double 5-pointed star with a meandering loop and star pattern surrounding to fill out the block.. The borders are stitched with a meandering star burst, resembling fireworks.

Hand-quilting suggestions. If you intend to use this quilt as a wall hanging or throw, quilt each block individually with a floral pattern or novelty motifs such as stars. Fill in the borders with a 2" cross hatch.

Quilt Top Assembly Diagram

Tip: The no pin method for making the square within a square unit

A fast way to make the square within a square unit (Figure 1) is to eliminate pinning. To do this, fold one red square in half, **right sides together**. Pinch with your fingers at the folded edge (Figure 2).

Figure 1

pinch

pinch

Figure 2

Next, fold one white triangle in half, **wrong sides together** and pinch along the bias edge, being careful not to stretch the bias (Figure 3). Repeat with 3 more triangles.

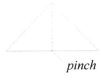

pinch

Figure 3

To sew units together, place 1 triangle on top of the square, wrong sides together, aligning the finger-pressed marks. Stitch along the raw edge. Use a stiletto or your fingertips to hold the tip of the triangle closest to you on the square in proper alignment so it doesn't shift apart during sewing (Figure 4). Press the triangle to the outside and repeat on the opposite side.

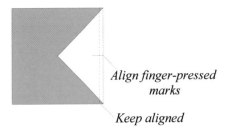

Align finger-pressed marks

Keep aligned

Figure 4

Finger press the remaining 2 sides of the square (Figure 5). Sew the remaining 2 triangles to the square. Press.

pinch

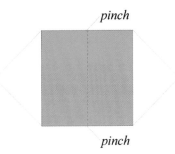

pinch

pinch

Figure 5

Chapter 6

Thrifty Wife

The *Thrifty Wife* block offers surprises depending on fabric placement and setting choice. In **Grapefruit Juice and Sugar**, the blocks are set on point, rendering them almost invisible. One has to look hard to see the block. At the end of the chapter, look for the tip *Easy interfacing appliqué* to make appliquéing the center circles of this block fast and easy.

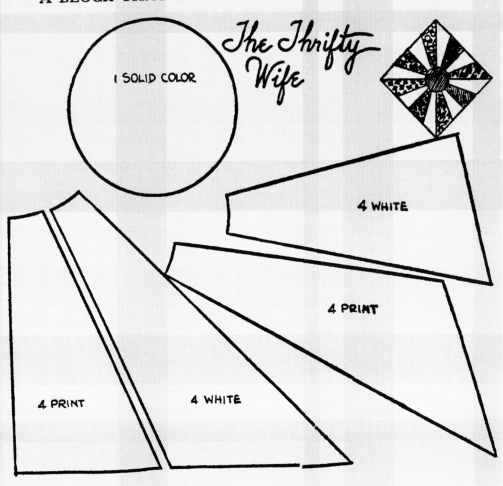

The Thrifty Wife block—Originally published May 10, 1939.

Single block instructions

Thrifty Wife
Finished block size: 12"

This block is constructed using 2 templates to make 16 "blades" that form the block. A circle is appliquéd to the center. Refer to these instructions when making the quilt described in this chapter or make the single block for a sampler quilt.

Fabric requirements

- Red: for a scrappy look, choose 8 different prints, 9" square each OR 8 fat eighths. For a controlled look, choose 1 fat quarter in 1 print.
- White: 1 fat quarter
- Blue solid: 1 scrap 4" square

Note: Because of the bias edges in this block, heavily starch the fabric before cutting.

Additional supplies
- Template plastic
- Spray starch
- Lightweight fusible interfacing
- Water soluble glue stick
- Invisible thread or thread to match appliqué fabric used in the center circle

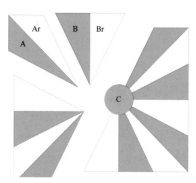

Block Assembly Diagram

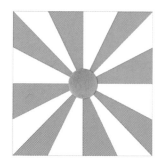

Block Diagram

Making the templates

1. Trace templates A and B onto the template plastic. Make sure to include the seam allowance and to draw the grain line arrow on the plastic.

Cut out the shapes on the solid line, being careful to make the edges smooth and accurate. Label the pieces A and B on the front side. To make the Ar and Br templates, turn the A and B templates over.

Cutting instructions

From red, cut
- 4 triangles from template A. Line up the grain line arrow with the grain line of the fabric. Cut with a rotary cutter, being careful not to cut into the template.
- 4 triangles from template B.

From white, cut
- 4 triangles from the Ar template.
- 4 triangles from the Br template.

From blue, cut
- 1—4 1/2" square (C)

Preparing the shapes for appliqué
Refer to *Easy interfacing appliqué* on page 91 and prepare 1 appliqué circle, using the blue 4 1/2" square and template C.

Piecing the block

1. Lay out the block as it will look once sewn, as shown in the *Block Assembly Diagram*. Pay attention to color placement so the block is stitched correctly.

2. Place a red triangle (A) right sides together with a white triangle (Ar). Sew along the long edge, starting at the outside and sewing toward the point. Be careful not to stretch the bias edges. Press. *Note:* Consistent pressing is the key to successfully piecing this block. Always press toward the dark fabric. Repeat to make 4 units.

3. Place a red triangle (B) right sides together with a white triangle (Br). Sew along the long edge, starting at the outside and sewing toward the point. Be careful not to stretch the bias edges. Press. Repeat to make 4 units.

4. Sew A units to B units. Press. Sew these units together to create two halves of the block. Pin halves together starting at the outside and working toward the center. Be sure to offset the outside edges by 1/4" to allow for seam allowance. Press. *Note:* The center will be covered by the appliqué circle, so there is no need to match the seams exactly in the middle of the block.

5. Trim the fabric in the middle of the block to reduce bulk. Make sure the hole you cut is smaller than the appliqué circle.

6. Finger press the appliqué circle by folding it in half and pinching the edges. Repeat in the opposite direction. Use these marks to line up the circle in the center of the block. Baste and stitch down as desired.

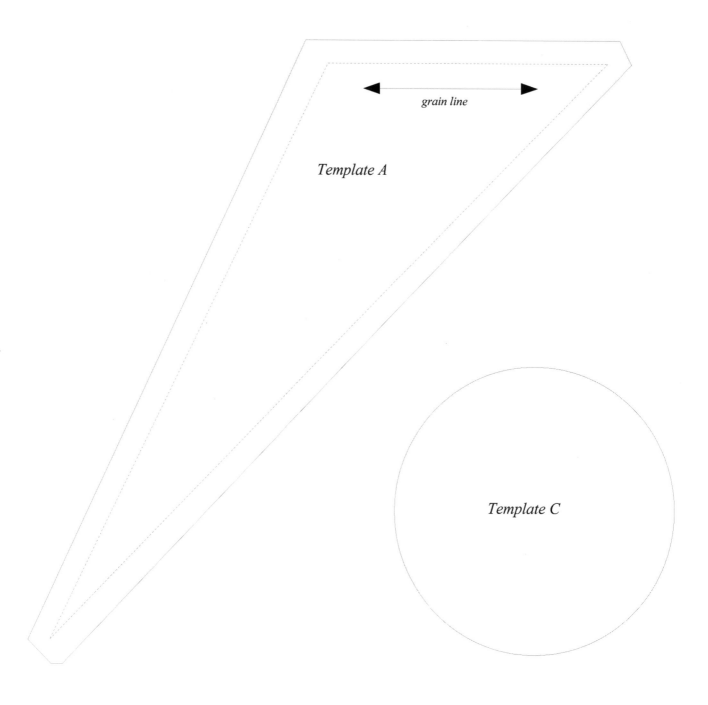

grain line

Template A

Template C

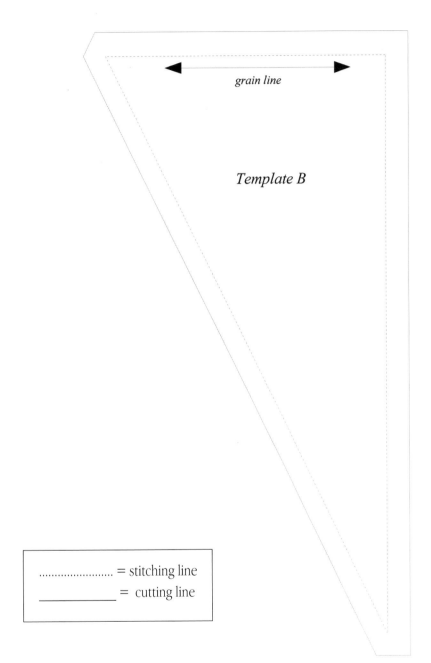

grain line

Template B

.... = stitching line
_____ = cutting line

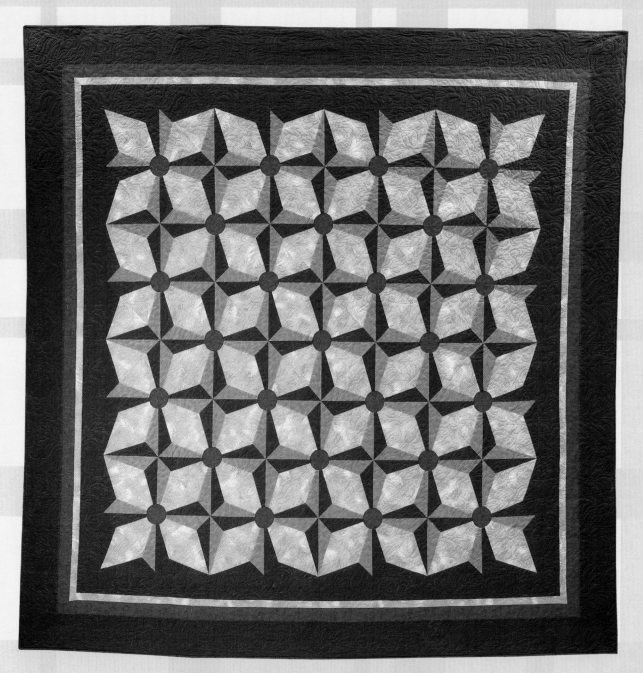

Grapefruit Juice and Sugar

91" x 91"

Pieced by Jenifer Dick, Harrisonville, Mo.

Quilted by Brenda Weien, Ottawa, Kan.

How to drink grapefruit juice without making a sour face

Grandma was a whiz at making do. One story her children remember is about grapefruit juice and sugar. In the early 1930s when money was tight, some people accepted government help. Grandma's neighbors were one such family. As part of that program, they received some surplus food, called commodities.

The neighbor received some food through the program that her children wouldn't eat, so she shared some with Grandma. One of those items was grapefruit juice. Well, Grandma knew that a little bit of sugar makes many things much better, including the bitter tang of grapefruit juice. Her children loved the improved juice. One day, Grandma made the mistake of telling the neighbor what she did to get her kids to drink it, and they never received the grapefruit juice again.

Grapefruit Juice and Sugar
Block size: 12"

This quilt is made of 25 blocks set on point with no sashing. Pieced setting triangles and corner triangles complete the setting for the top. Three plain mitered borders frame the quilt: a dark green 3 1/2" inner border, a gold 1" inner border, a red 2" middle border and a dark green 5 1/2" outer border.

Fabric requirements

- Dark green: 5 1/2 yards
- Light green: 2 1/2 yards
- Gold: 3 1/2 yards
- Red: 2 1/2 yards (includes binding)
- Binding: cut 5—2" wide strips from the length of the 2 1/2 yards of red from above **after** cutting the border strips. This allows enough to make about 388" of binding. If you prefer, cut 2 1/2" wide strips for binding from the yardage.
- Batting: queen size (92" x 108")
- Backing: 2 3/4 yards 108" wide green backing fabric or 8 yards of 42/44" wide green fabric to match top.

Note: Because of the bias edges in this block, heavily starch the fabric before cutting.

Additional supplies
- Template plastic
- Spray starch
- Lightweight fusible interfacing
- Water soluble glue stick
- Invisible thread or thread to match appliqué fabric used in the center circles

To get the most out of the yardage, cut the following fabric first and set aside:
From **dark green**, cut
- 2 3/4 yards for inner and outer border
From **gold**, cut
- 6" x the full **length** of the fabric
From **red**, cut
- 10" x the full **length** of the fabric

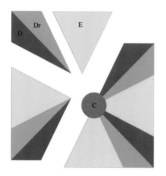

Block Assembly Diagram   *Block Diagram*

Making the templates

Trace templates D and E onto the template plastic. Make sure to add the seam allowance and to draw the grain line arrows on the plastic.

Cut out the shapes on the line, being careful to make the edges smooth and accurate. Label the pieces on the front side. To make the Dr template, turn template D over.

Blocks

Cutting instructions
From dark green, cut

- 6 strips—6 1/2" x the full **length** of fabric. Stack strips up to 4 layers and use template D to cut 100 triangles (Figure 1), lining up the correct grain line mark on the template with the grain line on the fabric. Cut using a rotary cutter being careful not to cut into the template. Reserve the leftover strips for the setting and corner triangles.

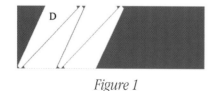

Figure 1

From light green, cut

- 6 strips—6 1/2" x the full **length** of fabric. Stack strips up to 4 layers and use template Dr to cut 100 triangles (Figure 2), lining up the correct grain line mark on the template with the grain line on the fabric. Cut using a rotary cutter being careful not to cut into the template. Reserve the leftover strips for the setting and corner triangles.

Figure 2

From gold, cut

- 4 strips—6 1/2" x the full **length** of fabric. Stack strips up to 4 layers and use template E to cut 100 triangles (Figure 3), lining up the correct grain line mark on the template with the grain line on the fabric. Cut, using a rotary cutter. Reserve the leftover strips for the setting and corner triangles.

Figure 3

From red, cut

- 25—4 1/2" squares

Preparing the shapes for appliqué

Refer to *Easy interfacing appliqué* on page 91 and prepare 25 appliqué circles, using the red 4 1/2" squares and Template C.

Piecing the blocks

Make 25 blocks, referring to the *Block*

Assembly Diagram and following the directions for piecing the single block on page 80. Pay attention to color placement so the blocks are stitched correctly. Press all blocks in the same direction.

Setting and corner triangles

Cutting instructions
From reserved dark green, cut*
- 16 D triangles. Line up the **setting triangle** grain line mark on the template with the grain line on the fabric.
- 16 Dr triangles. Line up the **setting triangle** grain line mark on the template with the grain line on the fabric.
- 12 more Dr triangles. This time, line up the **block** grain line mark on the template with the grain line on the fabric.

From reserved light green, cut*
- 12 Dr triangles. Line up the **block** grain line mark on the template with the grain line on the fabric.

From reserved gold, cut*
- 28 E triangles. Be sure to line up the correct grain line mark on the template with the grain line on the fabric.

*Because the grain lines are different on these triangles, make sure to clearly label each and lay out the appropriate triangle when piecing the setting and corner triangles.

Piecing the setting and corner triangles
1. Make 12 pieced setting triangles. Use 2 dark green triangles (D), 1 dark green and 1 light green triangle (Dr) and 2 gold triangles (E) for each setting triangle. Lay out fabrics, making sure the grain line for each triangle is in the correct position. Refer to the *Setting Triangle Assembly Diagram* for placement. Sew units together. Press all setting triangles in the same direction.

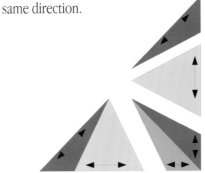

Setting Triangle Assembly Diagram

2. Make 4 pieced corner triangles. Use 1 dark green triangle (D), 1 dark green triangle (Dr) and 1 gold triangle (E) for each corner triangle. Lay out fabrics, making sure the grain line for each triangle is in the correct position. Refer to the *Corner Triangle Assembly Diagram* for placement. Sew units together. Press all setting triangles in the same direction.

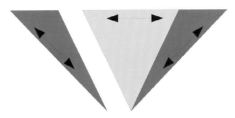

Corner Triangle Assembly Diagram

Borders

Inner and outer dark green border
From the reserved 2 3/4 yards, cut
- 4 strips 4" x 78"
- 4 strips 5 1/2" x 96"

Inner gold border

From the reserved 6", cut

• 4 strips—1 1/2" x 80"

Middle red border

From the reserved 10", cut

• 4 strips—2 1/2" x 85"

Assembling the quilt top

Note: Press after every step that follows.

1. Make block strip units, using the *Quilt Top Assembly Diagram* as a guide. Sew 7 blocks together. Sew 2 corner triangles to each end.

Sew 5 blocks together. Sew 2 setting triangles to each end. Repeat to make 2 units. Sew 3 blocks together. Sew 2 setting triangles to each end. Repeat to make 2 units. Sew 2 setting triangles to either side of 1 block. Sew a corner triangle to one side of the block. Repeat to make 2 units.

2. Join rows together.

3. Referring to *Making mitered borders* on page 35, add the dark green inner borders to the sides of the quilt top. Add the inner borders to the top and bottom of quilt. Press after each border is added. Miter the corners.

4. Add the gold inner borders to the sides of the quilt top. Add the inner borders to the top and bottom of quilt. Miter the corners.

5. Add the red middle borders to the sides of the quilt top. Add the middle borders to the top and bottom of quilt. Miter the corners.

6. Add the dark green outer borders to the sides of the quilt top. Add the outer borders to the top and bottom of quilt. Miter the corners.

Quilting and finishing the quilt

If you are using 8 yards of 42/44" wide fabric for backing, trim selvedges. Cut into equal thirds, roughly 3 sections 96" long. Sew 3 panels together. Press.

Layer the backing, batting and top. Baste and quilt as desired or use the suggestions below. Once quilted, bind in red.

Quilt Top Assembly Diagram

Machine quilting suggestions. Our quilt was quilted with an allover pantograph to accentuate the graphic nature of the design. The pattern has spiky points, which resemble fire, complementing the gold fabric. Your long-arm quilter might offer additional suggestions.

Hand quilting suggestions. Quilt a large sun motif in the center of each block. Fill in behind each sun and out to the yellow border on the edges with a 2" cross hatch. Stitch the yellow border and red borders in the ditch on both sides. In the outer green border, quilt a double cable.

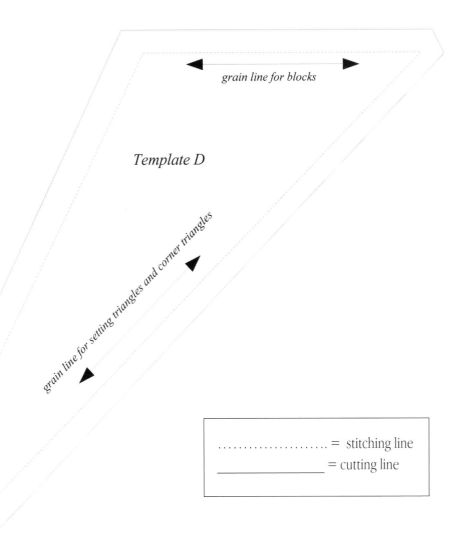

grain line for blocks

Template D

grain line for setting triangles and corner triangles

.... = stitching line

_____ = cutting line

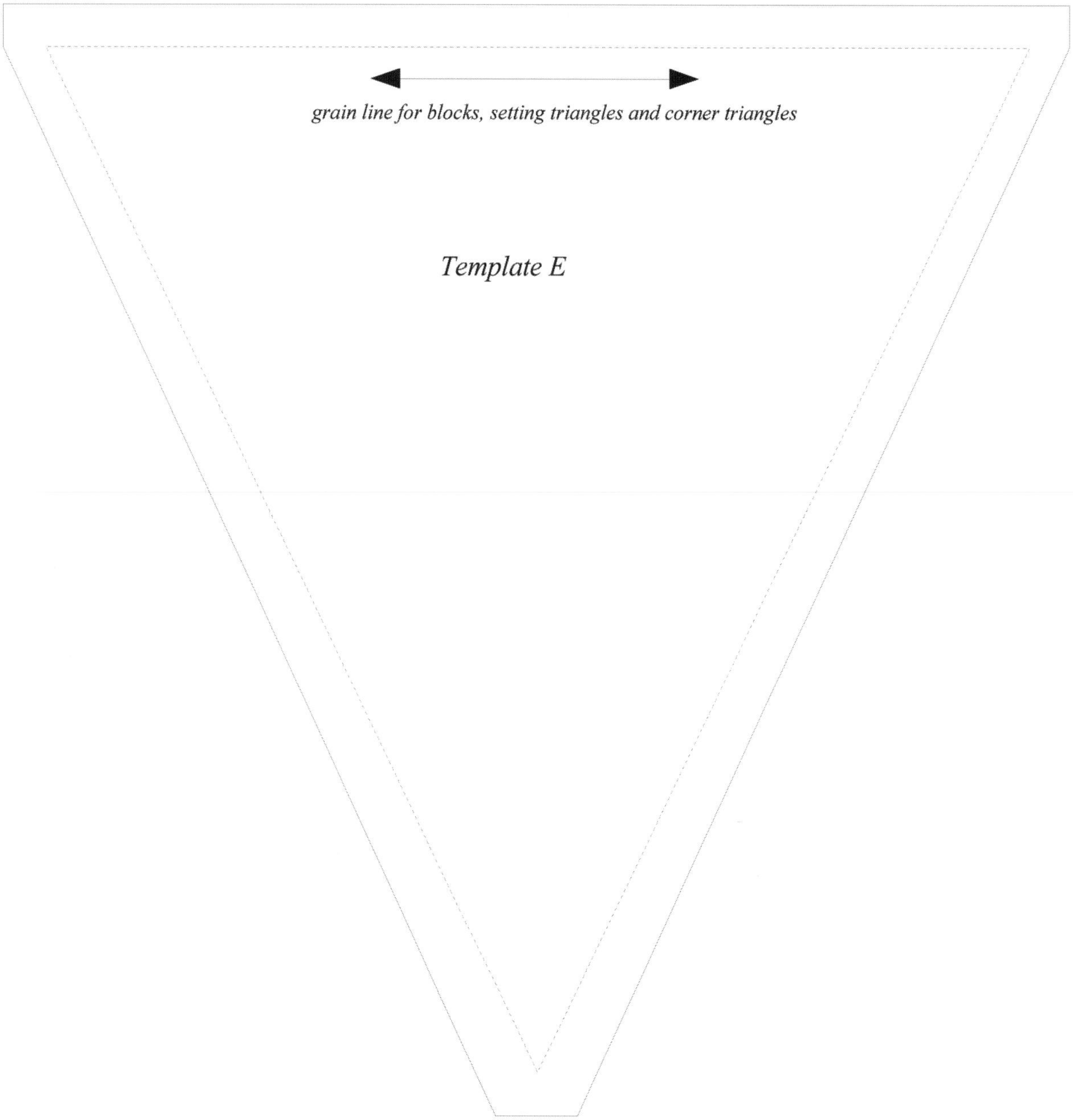

grain line for blocks, setting triangles and corner triangles

Template E

.... = stitching line

_____ = cutting line

Tip: Easy interfacing appliqué

An easy method of machine appliqué is to use a lightweight interfacing as a base for the appliqué shape. Because it is permanently pressed on the fabric, it does not have to be removed after sewing and because it is lightweight, it doesn't feel stiff in the finished quilt.

Supplies:
• Lightweight interfacing. See Sources on page 125.
• Water soluble glue stick
• Invisible thread or thread to match appliqué fabric

1. Draw or trace the appliqué shape on the non-fusible side of the interfacing. Cut out the shape on the line, being careful to make the edges smooth and accurate.

2. Place the interfacing shape, fusible side down, on the wrong side of the fabric. Refer to the manufacturer's directions. Cut out the appliqué shape leaving a scant 1/4" seam allowance.

3. Glue the seam allowance in place by running a ring of glue around the seam allowance and on to the outer edge of the interfacing. Use your fingers to fold the seam allowance over the appliqué shape. Check the front side of the shape to make sure the edges are smooth. You can reposition the seam allowance if necessary before the glue dries.

4. Position the shape on the block. Use the glue stick to glue around the inside edge on the underneath side of the shape to hold it in place or baste it with thread.

5. There are several options for sewing the shape onto the block. Experiment to see what works best for you:
• Use invisible thread and a zigzag stitch.
• Use thread that matches the appliqué fabric and a blind hem stitch.
• Use black thread and a buttonhole stitch.
• Use invisible thread or thread to match the color of the fabric. Sew in a straight line close to the edge of the appliqué shape.

After stitching, pull the top thread to the back and clip, leaving about a 1/4" tail.

Gay Patch Quilt.

657

BY alternating fabrics you can create a varied effect in the heirloom quilt. The "square dance" design takes only four fabrics for the 2-patch quilt. Pattern 815. Print plainly your name, address, zone and pattern number. Allow 10 days for delivery, by mail only. Send 25 cents in coin (no stamps) to The Kansas City Star, P. O. Box 161, Old Chelsea station, New York 11, N. Y. Please use this exact address.

657

USE scraps to make a simple quilt for your guest bedroom. The quilt design requires three patches. Pattern 657 includes information on yardage. Write plainly your name, address, zone and pattern number. Send 25 cents in coin, no stamps, to The Kansas City Star, 393 Needlecraft department, Box 161, N. Y. Old Chelsea station, New York 11, N. Y. Please use this exact address. Allow 10 days for delivery.

877

Craft projects are sketched here. The (left) is made by pattern 752. It's cross stitch. All sizes are included. The quilt (upper right) requires three Sun Bonnet girls and flower (lower) are favorites for towels. Pattern 877 initials are three sheets. To order, send 25 cents for each city Star, 393 Needlecraft department, New York 11, N. Y.

Picture These In Your Home

3136

127

3310

9363—The Wedding Ring Tile is a much loved favorite through the years and a wonderful way to use all those odds and ends of material scraps. Cutting guides, yardage estimates and other information included.

9363

Chapter 7

The Whirling Blade

The *Whirling Blade* block provides an excellent example of old-time tradition meeting modern art. In the **Box of Scraps** quilt, value and color combine forces to create a beautiful wall hanging rivaling any modern art piece. Look for the tip, *How to make quarter-square triangle units*, at the end of the chapter.

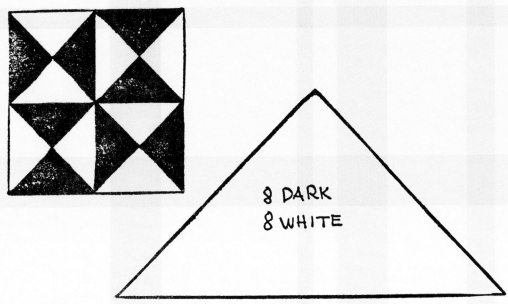

THE WHIRLING BLADE.

8 DARK
8 WHITE

The Whirling Blade block—Originally published March 8, 1944. Said <u>The Star</u>:
The design for the Whirling Blade quilt block was originated by Miss Luella Waggoner,
Fay, Oklahoma. One-tone pieces of contrasting color produce the illusion of whirling more
effectively that prints.

Single block instructions

The Whirling Blade
Finished block size: 6"

This block is constructed of 4 quarter-square triangle units sewn together as a four-patch block. Refer to these instructions when making the quilt described in this chapter or make the single block to include in a sampler quilt.

Fabric requirements
• White: 1 fat quarter
• Red: 1 fat quarter

Cutting instructions
From white, cut
• 2—4 1/4" squares
From red, cut
• 2—4 1/4" squares

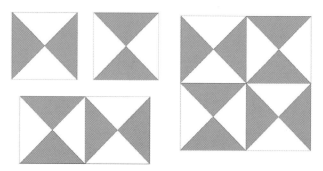

Block Assembly Diagram   *Block Diagram*

Piecing the block

1. Referring to *How to make quarter-square triangle units* on page 101, make 4 quarter-square triangle units using 2 red and 2 white squares. Trim units to 3 1/2".

2. Make the block. Lay out the block as it will look once sewn as shown in the *Block Diagram*. Pay attention to value placement so the block is stitched correctly.

3. Sew as a four-patch unit, as shown in the *Block Assembly Diagram. Note:* To ease construction and to alleviate bulk where the seams cross, it is important to press all the seams open in this block.

In the late '30s and early '40s, Grandma made comforters, rather than pieced quilts. These were tied on a frame similar to this one. My dad, Donald, remembers the frame set up in the yard so the neighborhood ladies and older girls could tie the quilts as the younger children played underneath the frame.

Box of Scraps

63" x 73"

Pieced and quilted by Mariya Drechsel, Freeman, Mo.

My Grandmother taught me to quilt—sort of

I remember vividly the day Grandma gave me a small cardboard box full of fabric when I was about 7 years old. In it were neatly stacked 2" squares of every color imaginable. There must have been 300 squares in the box.

She showed me how to sew the squares together by hand. This had to have been quite an undertaking because my hands were accustomed to holding bicycle handles, not needles and thread. I guess I sewed three or four of the squares together before I lost interest and ran off to play, but at the end of the day the box went home with me, where it found a permanent home in my closet. Occasionally, I'd get the box out and look at the fabrics, but no more of the precious scraps were ever sewn together. I don't know what happened to that box, but I wish I had it today.

Box of Scraps

Block size: 6"

This quilt is made of 63 Whirling Blade blocks in a straight set. Three borders frame the top: a plain blue 3" inner border, a pieced 1 1/2" middle border and a plain blue 6" outer border.

Fabric requirements

The richness of this quilt is in its use of a variety of fabrics. Our quilt includes 126 fabrics with no repeats, to give it a true scrappy look. For your quilt, choose at least 50 to 75 different fabrics. If you have repeats, be sure to sprinkle them evenly over the entire top. Make sure you use all colors and have roughly equal amounts of lights, mediums and darks to get the gradated feel. Don't forget black.

- Scraps:
  - Minimum: 50-75 fat eighths or scraps equal to two 4 1/2" squares. *Note:* leftover scraps will be used to create the middle border.
  - Maximum: 126 fat eighths or scraps equal to two 4 1/2" squares
- Blue: 2 yards
- Backing: 4 yards of 42/44" wide blue to match the top.
- Batting: twin size (72" x 90")
- Binding: 1/2 yard blue. This allows for 8—2" wide strips to make about 300" of binding. If you prefer 2 1/2" wide strips for binding, purchase 2/3 yard.

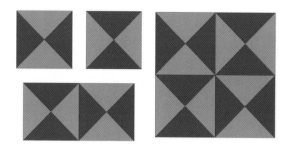

Block Assembly Diagram   *Block Diagram*

Cutting instructions

Blocks
From each fabric, cut
- 2—4 1/4" squares

Inner pieced borders
From 72 fabrics, cut
- 1—2" x 3 1/2" strips for the inner pieced border. You should have 72 strips.

From a black scrap, cut
- 4—2" squares for cornerstones on the inner pieced border.

Piecing the blocks
1. To achieve a gradated look, pair up 2 fabrics for each block that have low contrast. For example, match a dark and medium blue for one block and a medium and light yellow for another, etc.

Among the 63 blocks, there should be a wide range of values with approximately 20 light, 20 medium and 20 dark blocks whose values gradually fade into the next. Value is more important than color in this quilt.

2. Referring to *How to make quarter-square triangle units* on page 101, make 4 quarter-square triangle units using 2 light and 2 dark squares. Trim to 3 1/2". Press seams open.

Borders
Inner border

From blue, cut
- 2—3 1/2" x 54 1/2" strips from the **length** of the fabric.
- 2—3 1/2" x 48 1/2" strips from the **length** of the fabric.

Middle pieced border
1. Sew 20 strips together, end to end, to make 1 side border. Press. Repeat to make 2 side borders.

2. Sew 16 strips together, end to end, to make the top border. Press. Repeat to make the bottom border. Sew 2 black squares on either end of the top and bottom border. Press.

3. You should have pieced borders approximately the following lengths:
- 2—1 1/2" x 60 1/2" strips
- 2—1 1/2" x 51 1/2" strips

Outer border
From blue, cut
- 4—6 1/2" x 63 1/2" strips

Assembling the quilt top

Referring to the *Quilt Top Assembly Diagram*, lay out blocks and borders.

1. To get the gradated effect, arrange the blocks on a design wall. Experiment with different layouts. Our quilt is not only gradated by value with the lighter values toward the center, but the colors are grouped together as well. This gives the quilt a gentle flow from the dark to light values.

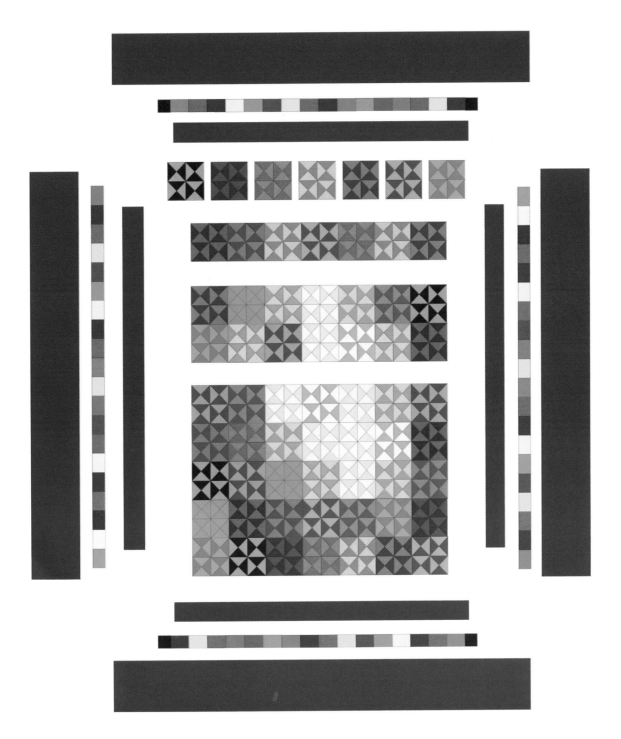

Quilt Top Assembly Diagram

Note: If you don't have a design wall, you can make one by pinning a table cloth that has a fleece backing to the wall with the backing side out. Place your blocks directly on the backing—there is no need to pin.

2. Once the layout is determined, sew the blocks together in rows, making sure to press all the seams open to avoid bulk where 4 blocks join together. Join the rows together. Press the seams open.

3. Add the long blue inner borders to the sides of the quilt. Add the short inner borders to the top and bottom of the quilt.

Note: Press after each border is added.

4. Add the long pieced middle border to the sides of the quilt. Add the short pieced borders top and bottom of the quilt.

5. Add blue outer borders to the sides of the quilt. Add the remaining borders to the top and bottom of the quilt.

Quilting and finishing the quilt

1. Trim selvedges off backing fabric. Cut into equal halves, roughly 2 yards each. Sew the 2 panels together.

2. Layer the backing, batting and top. Baste and quilt as desired or use the suggestions below. Once quilted, bind in blue to match the outer border.

Machine quilting suggestions. Our quilt was quilted in large spiral curves radiating from the center of the quilt to emphasize the rotating movement of the pinwheel in each block. Stipple quilting fills every other spoke of the spiral. The borders are quilted in slanted straight lines about 3" apart radiating out from the center.

Hand quilting suggestions. Sew around each quarter-square triangle 1/4" from the edge. Change thread to match the value of each shape. Sew the borders in a 3" cross-hatch on point.

Tip: How to make quarter-square triangle units

The bias edges in the traditional method for making quarter-square triangle units can make construction tricky. This method reduces the stretch on the bias edges making a stable unit.

The formula to remember: add 1 1/4" to the desired **finished** size. This is the size to cut the squares of fabric. For example, if you need a finished 3" quarter-square triangle unit, then the formula will be: 3"+1 1/4" = 4 1/4".

You can also make the units slightly bigger, then trim them to size after pressing. The advantage to making the units bigger is **accuracy**. Unless you sew exactly on the lines with no fabric shifting, it's tricky to get the correct size. By trimming the unit down after sewing, you're guaranteed to get the correct size.

The disadvantage: you have an added step of sizing the squares. Also, you will use more fabric, which can throw off your fabric requirements.

If you do choose to make the blocks bigger and trim to size, increase the cut square size by 1/4" to 1/2".

To make two 3" finished quarter-square triangle units

1. Cut two squares, one light and one dark, 4 1/4" (finished size + 1 1/4"). Determine if you want to cut to size or cut over-sized for trimming later. If you choose to make larger blocks, cut the two squares 4 1/2".

2. Draw a line diagonally from corner to corner on the back side of the lighter fabric (Figure 1).

3. Place 2 squares right sides together, aligning all 4 corners. Stitch 1/4" away from the drawn line on each side (Figure 2). Repeat with the remaining squares.

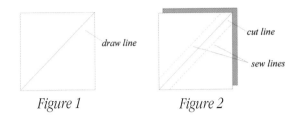

Figure 1   *Figure 2*

4. Cut apart on the drawn line. Press seams **open**.

5. Draw a line diagonally from corner to corner on the back side of 2 of these units (Figure 3).

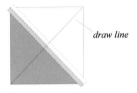

Figure 3

6. Place the two squares together with the opposite colors touching. Make sure the seams butt up together snugly. Pin if desired. Stitch 1/4" away from drawn line on each side as above (Figure 4). Repeat with remaining squares.

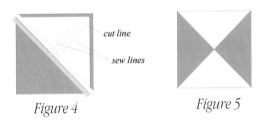

Figure 4   *Figure 5*

7. Cut apart on the drawn line. Press seams **open** (Figure 5).

8. If you're trimming, use the 45-degree line on an acrylic ruler as a guide and trim to the desired finished size plus seam allowance. In this case, you'll trim to 3 1/2."

Chapter 8

The Ratchet Wheel

The Ratchet Wheel block is a versatile block with chameleon qualities. When set together in a straight set, as seen in **A Wife of Noble Character**, the secondary pattern overshadows the original block, making it seem like a entire new pattern. Using different color placement as in **Couch Quilt**, the block takes on yet another personality, that of a distinct cross. Look for the tip, *Documenting your quilts*, at the end of this chapter.

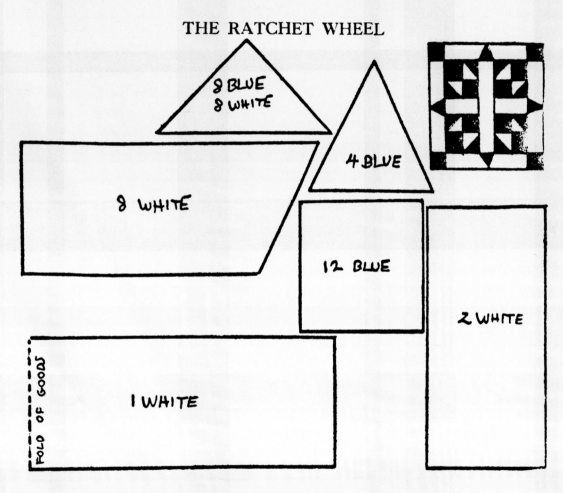

THE RATCHET WHEEL

8 BLUE
8 WHITE

4 BLUE

8 WHITE

12 BLUE

2 WHITE

1 WHITE

FOLD OF GOODS

The Ratchet Wheel block—Originally published March 5, 1947. Said <u>The Star</u>:
An advantage in this impressive design is the fact that it can be developed in any set of two-tone materials, or a combination of plain and print blocks.

Single block instructions

The Ratchet Wheel
Finished block size: 12"

This block is constructed similarly to a nine-patch with a pieced border framing the block. The 4 corner units are pieced four-patches made from half-square triangle units. Refer to these instructions when making the quilt described in this chapter, or make the single block for a sampler quilt.

Fabric requirements
- Blue: 1 fat quarter
- White: 1 fat quarter

Cutting instructions
From blue, cut
- 12—2" squares (A)
- 4—2 3/8" squares (B)
- 1—4 1/4" square (E). Cut the square in half diagonally twice to make 4 quarter square triangles.

From white, cut
- 4—2 3/8" squares (B)
- 4—2" x 5 3/8" strips (C). These strips will be cut at a 45-degree angle (Figure 1). Stack up to 4 strips right sides up. Line up the 45-degree angle on a ruler along the long side of the strips. Trim the 45-degree angle off the end of the strip.

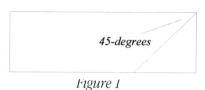

Figure 1

- 4—2" x 5 3/8" strips (D). Cut these strips to make a 45-degree angle. Be sure you cut the 45-degree angle in a mirror image of the (C) strips (Figure 2).

Figure 2

- 1—3 1/2" x 9 1/2" strip (F)
- 2—3 1/2" squares (G)

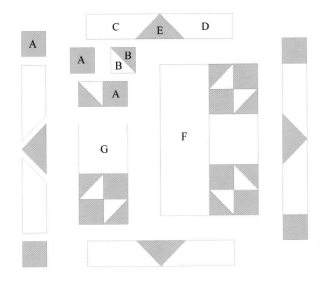

Block Assembly Diagram

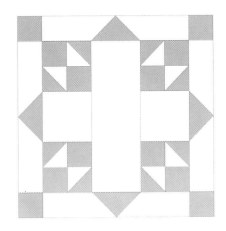

Block Diagram

Piecing the block

1. Referring to *How to make half-square triangle units* on page 45, make 8 half-square triangles using 4 blue and 4 white squares (B). Trim units to 2".

2. Make the block. Lay out the block as it will look once sewn as shown in the *Block Diagram*. Pay attention to color placement so the block is stitched correctly.

3. Sew 4 four-patch units using 2 half-square triangle units and 2 blue squares (A). Press.

4. Sew 2 four-patch units to either side of 1 white square (G), making sure the half-square triangle units are in the proper position. Press. Repeat with the remaining units. Sew these to either side of the long white strip (F). Press.

5. Sew the strip (C) to the triangle (E). Remember to offset the two by 1/4" so the strip will line up correctly (Figure 3). Press. Sew the strip (D) to the opposite side of the triangle (E). Press. Repeat to make 4 strips.

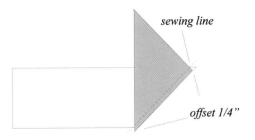

Figure 3

6. On 2 of the strips, sew the remaining 2 blue squares (A) to either end. Press. Join the short strips to the center of the block. Press. Join the 2 long strips on the top and bottom. Press.

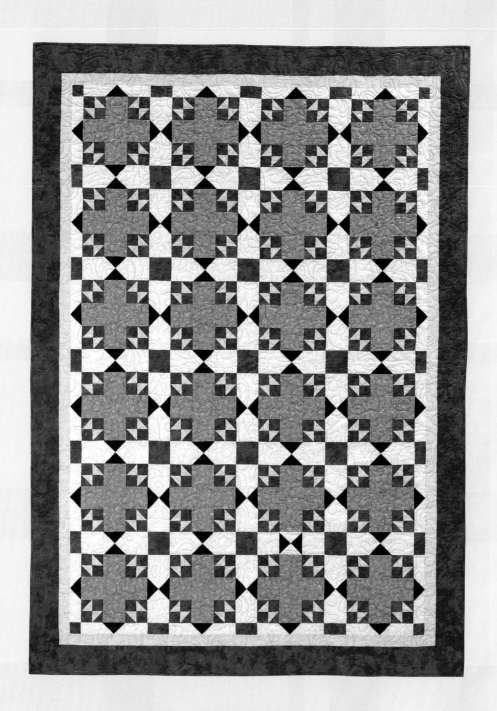

A Wife of Noble Character

58" x 81"

Pieced by Jenifer Dick, Harrisonville, Mo.

Quilted by Denise Hester, Parkville, Mo.

Give me that old-time religion

It can't go unsaid that Grandma was a faithful woman, and her life reflected that. She often read the Bible and attended Sunday services regularly, but also put her faith into daily practice in the way she lived her life and treated others. No words can sum up her life better than these.

> A wife of noble character who can find?
> She is worth far more than rubies.
> Her husband has full confidence in her
> and lacks nothing of value.
> She brings him good, not harm,
> all the days of her life.
> She sets about her work vigorously;
> her arms are strong for her tasks.
> She is clothed with strength and dignity;
> she can laugh at the days to come.
> She speaks with wisdom,
> and faithful instruction is on her tongue.
> She watches over the affairs of her household
> and does not eat the bread of idleness.
> Her children arise and call her blessed;
> her husband also, and he praises her:
> 'Many women do noble things,
> but you surpass them all.'
> Charm is deceptive,
> And beauty is fleeting;
> But a woman who fears the Lord is to be praised.
> *Proverbs 31:10-12, 17, 25-30*

A Wife of Noble Character

Block size: 12"

This quilt is made of 24 blocks set in a straight set.

Two borders frame the quilt: a plain yellow 1 1/2" inner border and a plain dark blue 4" outer border.

Fabric requirements

- Dark blue: 2 1/2 yards
- Medium blue: 1 1/4 yards
- Light blue: 1 3/4 yards
- Yellow: 1 1/3 yards
- Black: 1/2 yard
- Batting: twin size (72" x 90")
- Backing: 3 1/2 yards of 42/44" wide light blue to match the top.
- Binding: 1/2 yard color of your choice. This allows for 8—2" wide strips to make about 300" of binding. If you prefer 2 1/2" wide strips for binding purchase 2/3 yard.

To get the most out of the yardage, cut the following fabrics first and set aside:
From the **yellow** fabric, cut
- 1/2 yard for inner border
From the **dark blue** fabric, cut
- 1 yard for outer border

Blocks

Cutting instructions
From dark blue, cut
- 288—2" squares (A)
- 96—2 3/8" squares (B)

From medium blue, cut
- 24—3 1/2" x 9 1/2" strip (F)
- 48—3 1/2" squares (G)

From light blue, cut
- 96—2" x 5 3/8" strips (C). These strips will be cut at a 45-degree angle (Figure 1). Stack up to 4 strips right sides up. Line up the 45-degree angle on a ruler

along the long side of the strips. Trim the 45-degree angle off the end of the strip.

- 96—2" x 5 3/8" strips (D). Cut these strips to make a 45-degree angle. Be sure to cut the 45-degree angle to make a mirror image of the (C) strips (Figure 2).

From yellow, cut

- 96—2 3/8" squares (B)

From black, cut

- 24—4 1/4" square (E). Cut each square in half diagonally **twice** to make 4 quarter square triangles.

Piecing the blocks

1. Referring to *How to make half-square triangle units* on page 45, make 192 half-square triangles using 4 blue and 4 yellow squares (B). Trim units to 2".

2. To make the 24 blocks, follow the directions for piecing the single block found at the beginning of this chapter. Refer to the *Block Diagram* for color placement. *Note:* To ease construction of the quilt top, press the outer strip on the block toward the center on half of the blocks and press toward the outside on the other half.

Block Diagram

Borders

Inner border

Using the reserved **yellow** fabric, cut 7 strips 2" x the

full width of the fabric. From these, piece 4 border strips and cut to the following sizes:

- 2 strips—2" x 72 1/2"
- 2 strips—2" x 51 1/2"

Outer border

Using the reserved **blue** fabric, cut 7 strips 4 1/2" x the full width of the fabric. From these, piece 4 border strips and cut to the following sizes:

- 2 strips—4 1/2" x 75 1/2"
- 2 strips—4 1/2" x 59 1/2"

Assembling the quilt top

Referring to the *Quilt Top Assembly Diagram*, lay out blocks in 6 rows of 4 blocks each. Make sure to alternate the two different styles of pressed blocks to ease construction.

1. Sew blocks together in rows. Press. Join the rows together. Press.

2. Add the short yellow inner borders to the sides of the quilt top. Add the long inner borders to the top and bottom of quilt. *Note:* press after each border is added.

3. Add the short dark blue outer borders to the sides of the quilt top. Add the long dark blue outer borders to the top and bottom of quilt.

Quilting and finishing the quilt

1. Trim selvedges from the 3 1/2 yards of backing fabric. Cut into 2 equal pieces, roughly 63" long each. Sew 2 panels together. Press.

2. Layer the backing, batting and top. Baste and quilt

as desired or use the suggestions below. Once quilted, bind it in the fabric of your choice.

Machine quilting suggestions. Our quilt was quilted with an all-over design as not to diminish the graphic nature of the design. It is a spiky pattern to emphasize the points of the triangles in the top. Consult with your long-arm quilter for more quilting ideas.

Hand quilting suggestions. Stitch in the ditch around the triangles, the light blue units and large cross in each block. Within the cross, quilt a formal floral motif. In the blue square created when four blocks are joined together, quilt a floral motif to match the one used in the cross. In the inner border, sew 1" squares on point. On the outer border, stitch the same floral as used in the cross.

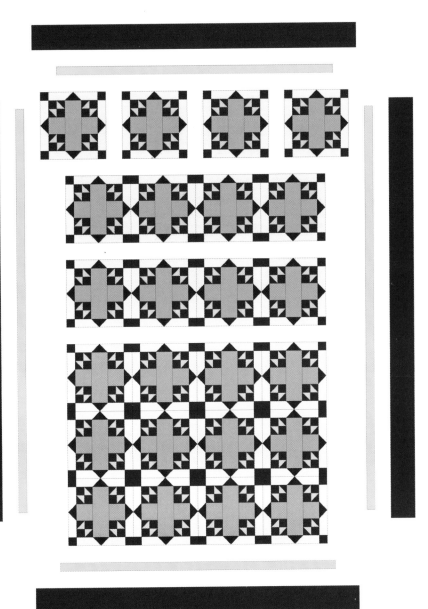

Quilt Top Assembly Diagram

Couch Quilt

64" x 40"

Pieced and quilted by Dianne Barnden, Wellington, New Zealand

Couch Quilt

Block size: 8"

Made to go over the back of a couch, this quilt needs only 5 blocks. The blocks are separated by a black 1" sashing and medium tan 1" cornerstones. Three borders frame the quilt: a large plain burgundy uneven inner border, a plain black 1" middle border and a plain burgundy 2" outer border.

Fabric requirements

- Burgundy: 2 yards
- Medium tan: 1/2 yard
- Cream: 1/2 yard
- Black: 1/2 yard
- Batting: throw size (60" x 70")
- Backing: 2 yards of dark fabric to match top
- Binding: 1/2 yard burgundy to match outer border. This allows for 6—2" wide strips to make about 230" of binding. If you prefer 2 1/2" wide strips for binding purchase 2/3 yard.

To get the most out of the yardage cut the following fabrics first and set aside:

From the **burgundy** fabric, cut
- 31" x the full **length** of fabric for inner and outer borders.

From the **black** fabric, cut
- 8" x the full **width** of fabric for middle border.

Blocks

Cutting instructions
From burgundy, cut
- 5—3 1/4" square (E). Cut each square in half diagonally, twice to make 4 quarter square triangles.
- 5—2 1/2" x 6 1/2" (F)
- 10—2 1/2" squares (G)

From medium tan, cut
- 20—1 1/2" x 3 7/8" strips (C). These strips will be cut at a 45-degree angle (Figure 1). Stack up to 4 strips right sides up. Line up the 45-degree angle on a ruler along the long side of the strips. Trim the 45-degree angle off the end of the strip.
- 20—1 1/2" x 3 7/8" strips (D). Cut strips to make a 45-degree angle. Be sure you cut the 45-degree angle to make a mirror image of the (C) strips (Figure 2).
- 12—1 1/2" squares for cornerstones

From cream, cut
- 60—1 1/2" squares (A)
- 20—1 7/8" squares (B)

From black, cut
- 20—1 7/8" squares (B)
- 16—1 1/2" x 8 1/2" strips for sashing

Piecing the blocks

1. Referring to *How to make half-square triangle units* on page 45, make 40 half-square triangles using 4 cream and 4 black squares (B). Trim units to 1 1/2".

2. To make 5 blocks, use the directions for piecing the single block on page 104. Refer to the *Block Diagram* for color placement.

Borders
Inner border
Using the reserved **burgundy** fabric, cut
- 2 strips—6 1/2" x 10 1/2" for side inner borders

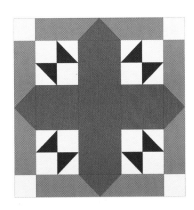

Block Diagram

- 1 strip—6 1/2" x 58 1/2" for bottom inner border
- 1 strip—18 1/2" x 58 1/2" for top inner border
- 2 strips—2 1/2" x 40 1/2" for side outer borders
- 2 strips—2 1/2" x 60 1/2" for top and bottom outer borders

Middle border

Using the reserved **black** fabric, cut 5 strips 1 1/2" x the full width of the fabric. From these, piece 4 border strips and cut to the following sizes:

- 2 strips—1 1/2" x 58 1/2" for top and bottom borders
- 2 strips—1 1/2" x 36 1/2" for side borders

Assembling the quilt top

Referring to the *Quilt Top Assembly Diagram*, lay out blocks, sashing strips and cornerstones.

1. Make block strip units and sashing units. Sew 6 sashing strips to 5 blocks. Press toward the sashing. Next, sew 6 cornerstones to 5 sashing strips. Press toward the sashing. Repeat to make a second sashing unit. Sew sashing units to either side of the block strip unit. Press.

2. Add the short burgundy inner borders to the sides of quilt. Add the long burgundy inner borders to the top and bottom of the quilt top. *Note:* Press after each border is added.

3. Add the long black middle borders to the top and bottom of quilt. Add the short black middle borders to the sides of the quilt top.

4. Add the long burgundy outer borders to the top and bottom of quilt. Add the short burgundy outer borders to the sides of the quilt top.

Quilting and finishing the quilt

Trim selvedges from backing fabric. Layer the backing,

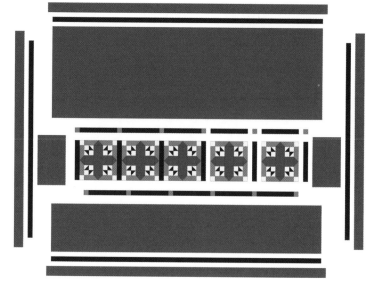

Quilt Top Assembly Diagram

batting and top. Baste and quilt as desired or use the suggestions below. Once quilted, bind in burgundy to match the outer border.

Machine quilting suggestions. Our quilt was quilted using straight line stitching with a walking foot on a regular sewing machine. The blocks are stitched in the ditch around the red cross that forms in the center of each block. Diagonal lines run from the corner to corner forming an X through each block. The center of the quilt is stitched in the ditch around the outer sashing.

The inner red border is stitched 1/4" from the black border around the perimeter of the quilt. A 3" cross hatch grid fills in the inner border, stitched in burgundy thread to match the fabric. The outer red border is stitched 1/4" from the black around the perimeter of the quilt.

Hand quilting suggestions. This quilt can be hand quilted in the same manner described for machine quilting. Or, use the large open spaces in the inner border to show off elaborate, fancy quilting.

Tip: Documenting your quilts

Because of my search for information about my grandmother's quilts, I am all too aware of the importance of labels. I have often wished she had put just the year on all her quilts. She did sign and date her first quilt. I wonder why she stopped after that? I am fortunate, however. I know when she made her first quilt and I know when she died so it's a little easier to date the rest. But what about the next generation? Once I'm gone, my children won't know this information first-hand and her quilts could be scattered throughout the Midwest.

This is why it's important to put a label on all of your quilts. If you took the time to make it, it deserves to be signed.

- Labels add value to your quilt. Provenance--the history and stories surrounding an antique--adds value to any quilt, and chances are at least some of your quilts will become antiques some day.

- Labels can include more information than you might tell the recipient. Non-quilters won't remember the block name, who quilted it, or even the date the quilt was made. A label records this information for the future.

- Labels provide future generations with information about the quilt maker. How many times have you seen a beautiful quilt at an antique store and thought, "If that quilt were made by my grandmother, I would never sell it." Well, that quilt **was** made by someone's grandmother and they just don't know it because it doesn't have her name on it. If you want your quilt to become a treasured heirloom, sign it.

- Labels let the future generations know why you made the quilt. All quilts tell a story, even the less than perfect ones! When you let others know the story behind the quilt, it becomes an expression of your love and personality.

What you put on the label is also important. The more information it includes, the more valuable your quilt could be in the future. At a minimum, include your name, the year the quilt was made and your city and state. But that's just the beginning. I usually also include my maiden name and the name of the quilt. From there, anything goes—put why you made the quilt, who you made it for, where you got the pattern, the pattern name, and who quilted it. Any information about the quilt is appropriate.

There are many ways to make a label. The easiest is to use a permanent fabric marker and write directly on the back of the quilt—no label necessary. From there, the sky's the limit. Here are just a few suggestions.

- Piece an additional block and embroider the information on it.
- Use a preprinted muslin label (available at most quilt shops) and write your information with a permanent fabric marker.
- Type the information on your computer and print it directly onto a muslin label.

Chapter 9

The Hen and Her Chicks

The Hen and Her Chicks block is a natural choice for a baby quilt. As seen in **Grandmother's Last Kiss**, a wide variety of fabrics makes the quilt exciting and colorful. The tip *Easy method for choosing fabrics* can help with fabric decisions.

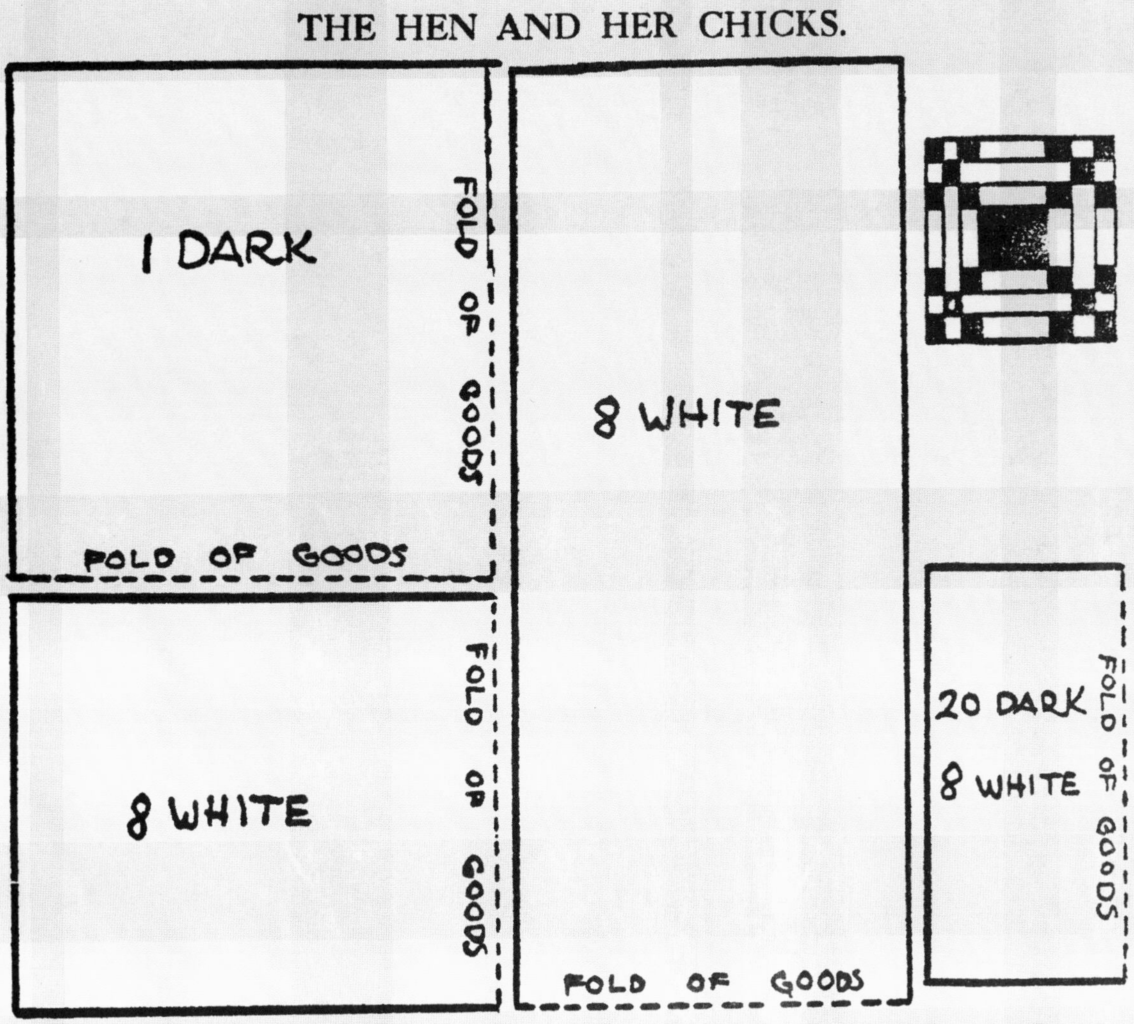

THE HEN AND HER CHICKS.

1 DARK

FOLD OF GOODS

FOLD OF GOODS

8 WHITE

8 WHITE

FOLD OF GOODS

FOLD OF GOODS

20 DARK

8 WHITE

FOLD OF GOODS

FOLD OF GOODS

The Hen and Her Chicks block—Originally published June 18, 1947. Said <u>The Star</u>:
This pattern is an original coming from Miss Iva Corbil, Route 3, Van Buren, Ark., who says she chose the name, "The Hen and Her Chicks," for it because of the large center square surrounded by smaller ones. One-tone materials would be more effective for this design than prints.

Single block instructions

The Hen and Her Chicks
Finished block size: 9"

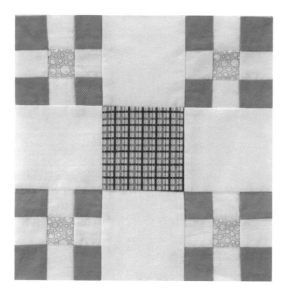

This block is constructed as a double nine-patch— it has 4 small nine-patches in the corners, 4 plain patches and a plain center patch different from the others. Refer to these instructions when making the two quilts described in this chapter or make the single block for a sampler quilt.

Fabric requirements
- White: 1 fat quarter
- Green plaid: 1 fat eighth
- Green solid: 1 fat eighth
- Yellow: 1 fat eighth

Cutting instructions
From white, cut
- 4—3 1/2" squares (B)
- 16—1 1/2" squares (A)
From green plaid, cut
- 1—3 1/2" square (C)
From green solid, cut
- 16—1 1/2" squares (A)
From yellow, cut
- 4—1 1/2" squares (A)

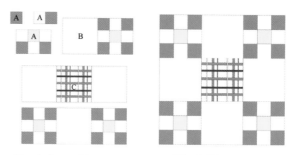

Block Assembly Diagram   *Block Diagram*

Piecing the block

1. Make 4—3 1/2" nine-patch blocks. You'll need 4 white squares (A), 4 green solid squares (A), 1 yellow square (A). Stitch together as shown in the *Block Assembly Diagram*. Sew units into 3 rows. Press. Sew completed rows together to complete the units. Press.

2. Lay out 4 small nine-patch units and 4 white squares (B) and 1 green plaid (B) as it will look once sewn as shown in *Block Diagram*.

3. Sew the block together as you would sew a simple nine-patch block, as described above.

Tip: Easy method for choosing fabrics

When a quilt requires many fabrics, such as "Grandmother's Kiss," the thought of picking a group of fabrics that go together can be confusing and intimidating. Here is a basic trick to make this process go smoothly with good results every time.

Fabric designers are experts in color theory. They know what colors work together. Tap into their experience and let them choose your fabric. When you're at the quilt shop, lay out a bolt of fabric that has multiple colors in it. Make sure the overall "feel" of the fabric is pleasing to you. Don't dissect each individual color yet. It may include your least favorite color, but all you're interested in is the overall impression of the fabric. This is now your focus fabric.

Using the focus fabric, you can choose all the others that will go in your quilt. First, match exactly the colors from the focus fabric. Spread all these out in a fan on top of the focus fabric and see what you think. Don't be afraid to use what you consider to be the least desirable color. I guarantee it will all blend in and look great, because it did in the focus fabric.

Make sure to choose a variety of prints and geometrics in several sizes and scale. Pick stripes and checks, florals and tone-on-tones in any combination that is pleasing to you. Be sure to pick dark, medium and light values. As long as the colors all come from your focus fabric, it will be fine. You'll easily be able to see what works and what doesn't. Ask other shoppers and the store employees for opinions, if you're stumped. But in the end, do what feels right for you.

Once your purchases are made, cut small 2" squares of each fabric and paste them on a piece of paper. Label the swatches to keep them organized. I give my fabrics names to help me remember where they go. These names are usually descriptive: yellow, blue, blue swirl, checks, border, etc. Nothing too creative is necessary here, this is just for your use.

Another advantage to having a swatch page is if you run out of one fabric, you have a reference to take back to the quilt shop. I often note the manufacturer and the color number next to the swatch in case my quilt shop is out and I have to search the internet for more.

Practice and experience will make picking colors easier, but using a focus fabric is a good way to start until you're ready to pick colors solo.

Grandmother's Last Kiss

38" x 48"

Pieced by Jenifer Dick, Harrisonville, Mo.

Quilted by the women of the United Methodist Quilters, Harrisonville, Mo.

Denniele Bohannon, Sis Buchholz, Lois Clement, Mildred Randall, Joyce Roach and Ellen Wray

Elevators—like life—go up and down

The last time I saw my Grandma was in the hospital when my Dad had cancer. In those days, children under age 12 couldn't be in the patient's rooms. For me, that meant long hours by myself in the waiting room putting puzzles together.

One of those days, Grandma came to visit Dad. She was visibly upset. I was all alone as usual when she emerged from his room. Her eyes were full of tears. She walked right passed me and pushed the button for the elevator. She hesitated for a second and looked back at me. She walked over to me with huge tears in her eyes. Even without consciously knowing it, I knew that Grandma never cried around other people. She kissed my forehead with a huge juicy kiss. "Be a good girl," was all she said. Next thing I knew, the elevator doors were closing with Grandma inside and I was alone again.

Looking back, I realize that couldn't have been the last time I saw her, because Dad had cancer in 1976 and she died in 1977. But that memory is so vivid, it has overshadowed all others and to this day, I still think of that as the last time I ever saw her.

Grandmother's Last Kiss

Block size: 9"

This quilt is made of 12 blocks separated by 1" sashing and cornerstones. Two borders frame the quilt: a 1/2" plain inner border and a 3" outer border with cornerstones.

Fabric requirements*
- Focus fabric: 1 3/4 yards
- Yellow background: 1 yard
- Orange: 1/2 yard
- Green stripe: 1/2 yard
- Blue swirl: 1 fat quarter
- Gold: 1 fat quarter
- Blue: 1 fat quarter
- Green: 1 fat quarter
- Binding: 1/3 yard orange to match inner border. This allows for 5—2" wide strips to make about 200" of binding. If you prefer 2 1/2" wide strips for binding, purchase 1/2 yard.
- Backing: 1 1/2 yards
- Batting: crib size (45" x 60")

Refer to Easy method for choosing fabrics *on page 117 for information on how to select fabrics for this quilt.*

Blocks

Cutting instructions
From focus fabric, cut
- 4—3 1/2" x full length of fabric strips. These will be cut to size later.
- 12—3 1/2" squares (C)

To allow for a directional print in the focus fabric, cut
- 2—3 1/2" x full width of fabric strips. These will be cut to size later.
- 2—3 1/2" x full length of fabric strips.

From yellow background, cut
- 48—3 1/2" squares (B)
- 192—1 1/2" squares (A)

From orange, cut
- 4—1 1/2" x the full length of fabric. These will be cut to size later.
- 96—1 1/2" squares (A)

From blue cut
- 48—1 1/2" squares (A)

From gold, cut
- 48—1 1/2" squares (A)

From green, cut
- 48—1 1/2" squares (A)

Piecing the blocks

To make the 12 blocks, use the directions for piecing the single block found at the beginning of this chapter. Pay attention to color placement as you sew, referring to the *Color Placement Diagram*.

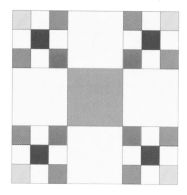

Color Placement Diagram

Sashing

Cutting instructions
From green stripe, cut
• 31—1 1/2" x 9" strips
From blue swirl, cut
• 20—1 1/2" squares

Borders

Inner border
Using the reserved orange strips, cut
• 2 strips—1" x 32 1/2"
• 2 strips—1 " x 41 1/2"

Outer pieced border

Cutting instructions
From reserved focus fabric strips, cut
• 2 strips cut from width—3 1/2" x 32 1/2"
• 2 strips cut from length—3 1/2" x 42 1/2"

From blue swirl, cut
• 4—3 1/2" squares

To make the pieced outer borders, sew 2 blue swirl squares to either end of the short focus fabric strips. Press. Repeat with the other short focus fabric strip.

Assembling the quilt top

1. Make block strip units and sashing units. Sew 4 sashing strips to 3 blocks. Press. Next, sew 4 cornerstones to 3 sashing strips. Press. Sew sashing unit to block strip unit. Press. Make 4 units.

2. Sew remaining cornerstones to sashing strips. Press. Sew to the bottom of one block strip unit. This will be the bottom row of the quilt.

3. Join rows together according to the *Quilt Top Assembly Diagram*. Press.

4. Add the long orange inner borders to the sides of the quilt top. Add the short orange inner borders to the top and bottom of the quilt. Press after each border is added.

5. Add the outer borders to the sides of the quilt top. Add the long pieced outer borders to the top and bottom of quilt. Press after each border is added.

Quilting and finishing the quilt

Layer the backing, batting and top. Baste and quilt as desired or use the suggestions below. Once quilted, bind in orange to match the inner border.

Machine quilting suggestions. If you plan on using this as a baby quilt or a quilt for a young child, the quilting should be strong and durable. Machine quilt in an all-over stipple or other pattern. Consider a whimsical pattern with a child's theme. Ask your quilter for suggestions.

Hand quilting suggestions. The quilt shown here was hand quilted with free-hand drawn stars in the open yellow squares. The small nine-patch units were quilted on the diagonal through each square. The blocks are stitched in the ditch all around. The inner border is stitched in the ditch around the entire perimeter of the quilt. The outer border has stitching evenly spaced, straight out from the inner border to the binding.

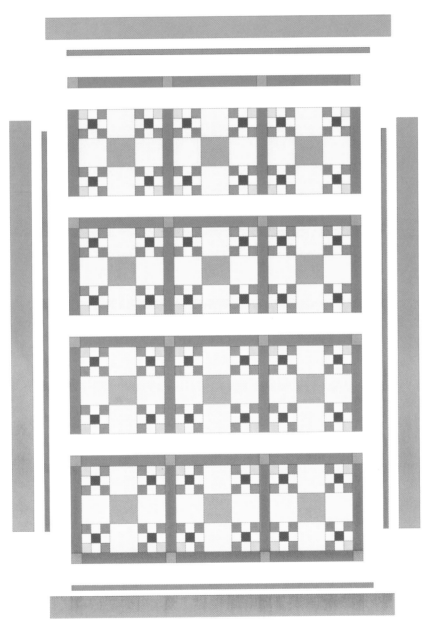

Quilt Top Assembly Diagram

How to use this book

Information on various aspects of quiltmaking are included in this section, and helpful tips are included in each chapter. In addition, each chapter has complete instructions for making one block. You may want to make only one block for a sampler or block swap.

Fabric

To get the best results for the life of your quilt, purchase 100% cotton, quilt shop quality fabric. Pre-wash it with a fade and bleed resistant solution, such as Retayne (see *Sources* on page 125). This will keep your fabrics from bleeding, fading or crocking—when color rubs off one fabric on to another.

It's a good idea to press your fabrics before storing them. If not, they may develop wrinkles that are hard to press out later. Then, press fabrics with spray starch before beginning a project, especially if there are bias edges in the block. Keep in mind that there will be about 40"-42" of usable width of the fabric after washing. Sometimes after straightening the fabric and trimming the edges, there can be even less. The quilts in this book are all based on 42/44" width fabric, assuming it will shrink to 40/42" after pre-washing. If your fabric shrinks to less than 40" wide, your yardage calculations might be off slightly.

Notions

The quilts in this book were all made using standard quiltmaking notions. Additional tools are used to aid in the making of a few of the quilts. These are noted in the corresponding chapters and in the *Sources* section on page 125.

Yardage

Although every effort has been made to ensure the fabric requirements are accurate, it never hurts to purchase more than listed. **I recommend buying at least 1/4 yard more.** It is inevitable that at some point you'll make the mistake of cutting 40 squares 2 1/2" x 2 1/4" instead of 2 1/2" x 2 1/2". My experience is that fabric can be like an antique. You should buy it when you see it, because it may not be there when you return. *Note:* A fat quarter measures 18" x 22". A fat eighth measures 9" x 22".

Make it larger than necessary and cut it down to size. All the patterns in this book are written to size—that is all the cutting measurements are exact. However, fabric requirements include enough extra to make particular units—such as half-square and quarter-square triangle units—larger than necessary so they can be cut down to size to ensure accuracy. If you choose to make a unit over-sized and trim, add 1/4" to 1/2" to the cutting measurements. For more on this, see *How to make half-square triangle units* on page 45.

Pressing

I believe pressing to be a very important part of quiltmaking. Properly pressed, a block will lay flat with no bulky seam intersections and will be the correct size. Your long-arm machine quilter will thank you for making her job easier.

As you make your blocks, press after each seam is sewn, paying attention to the direction you're pressing. For four- and nine-patch blocks, make sure the units have opposing seams so the points line up exactly when sewn.

For the borders, the typical rule is to press to the outside, but if there is a pieced border, you'll want to press away from it. Mitered borders are pressed toward the quilt top.

Press with a more up and down motion than side to side. Vigorous pressing will distort fabric. When pressing units with exposed bias edges, keep the tip of the iron as close to the sewn seam as possible and press in the direction of the grain line of the fabric. This will keep stretching to a minimum.

Pressing the seams to one side is the norm, but there are times when it makes sense to press seams open. One reason is to ease construction of a quilt with many seams—as seen in **Zip! There It Goes!** on page 27. Avoiding a bulky lump on the top is another reason to press seams open. This is illustrated in the **Box of Scraps** quilt on page 97.

Borders

All the patterns include the exact measurements for borders, but because your quilt top may have slight variations in size, cut the border strips a few inches longer than specified in the directions. Then use the guidelines in *Making pieced borders work* on page 61 and *Making mitered borders* on page 35 to determine the exact measurement for your borders.

Quilt backing

If you prefer plain, unpieced backing, there are two main fabric options—wide width or regular 42/44" width.

- **Wide-width backing**. Fabric is available in several widths to fit almost any size bed quilt. Wider fabric eliminates the need to piece backing and it is usually much cheaper than the narrow width option. Although there are many varieties, sometimes it is still difficult to match the colors used in the top of a quilt. Some fabric manufacturers produce backing to match specific fabric lines.
- **42/44" width backing.** If matching the colors used in the top is important to the integrity of your quilt, then it's best to purchase regular-width fabric. The biggest detriment to this, however, is cost. You can end up spending as much money on the backing as the top.

A word on muslin as a backing: although our foremothers used muslin for piecing and appliqué as well as backing, the quality of today's fabrics makes muslin my last choice for backing. Muslin is inexpensive, but it wears out faster and is quite plain to put on the back of a fine quilt. I prefer either a print or a dark backing on a quilt that will be used on a bed every day to hide spots.

Batting

Volumes have been written on batting. There are more varieties than can be counted. Again, batting is a matter of personal choice. Some quilters like high loft, some like their quilts as flat as a pancake. I suggest that when you see a quilt you like, ask the maker what batting was used. Ask your friends what they prefer and ask your long-arm quilter what she or he prefers to use. I guarantee they'll have an opinion. Take all these opinions into consideration and choose one. You'll make mistakes, but you'll soon learn which one works best for you in which quilt. I used to think all quilts had to be batted in cotton, but now I think polyester is best if the purpose of the quilt is to keep you warm in bed during the winter. Experience is the best teacher.

Binding

Binding should match your top in some form. It can match the outer border, making it disappear or it can match one of the accent colors used in the blocks, making it a design element. Make sure to purchase binding fabric when you purchase the rest of the fabrics. You could get into trouble if you get the top done and find you don't have enough to have a matching binding. All binding yardage is included in the pattern instructions.

Quilting

Quilting patterns are notorious for adding this sentence: Quilt as desired. This used to panic me so much that for years, I only made tops. As these piled up, I realized that as much as I love to piece, if I don't get them quilted, tops are not quilts. I knew hand-quilting wasn't for me and my feeble attempts to learn free motion quilting on my regular machine stressed me out too much. So, I went to my local quilt shop and picked up the business cards of several local long-arm quilters. I set up appointments to view their work and discuss pricing, schedules, and how to prepare the quilt top.

If you don't already have a good relationship with a long-arm quilter, I heartily recommend you find one. Make sure to interview a potential long arm quilter before you hand over your precious top. There are many excellent machine quilters who don't quilt in my style. No matter how many awards they win, if it's not my style, I won't be happy. So check them out thoroughly and ask many questions.

Each pattern in this book offers machine and hand quilting suggestions. Many times you'll know what you want, but other times a suggestion gives you a place to start.

Long-arm quilting. The quilts in this book are bold and graphic in design. This means that the quilting can, in many cases, be very subdued and simple. An allover pattern, called a pantograph, is a good choice for any of these quilts. A pantograph can be floral and flowing or sharp and angular to suit the personality of the quilt. Pantographs are more economical than custom quilting and in many cases just as beautiful. If you don't have a particular idea for the quilting, be sure to consult with your long-arm quilter for suggestions.

Hand quilting. Because I have limited hand-quilting experience, I usually recommend stitching in the ditch around the shapes or stitching 1/4" away from the seam. This is the most basic of hand quilting directions. An experienced quilter will know of other patterns to offset the piecing more elaborately.

However, these patterns were developed in the `30s and `40s when that was a popular form of quilting, so blocks look good quilted this way. Many of the quilts have open spaces for showing off fancy stitching. Look for these areas to showcase your skills.

Labels

Always label your quilts. At a minimum, put your name (including your maiden name), the date and your town and state. For more information on labels, see *Documenting your quilts* on page 113.

Sources

Any quilt shop can special order any of these products if they are not already in stock.

- *Retayne*—a color fixative for commercially dyed cotton fabrics. G&K Craft Industries, Ltd., Somerset, MA 02726-0038.

- *Tri-rec* tools by Darlene Zimmerman and Joy Hoffman. EZ Quilting, West Warren, MA 01092. This could be used instead of making templates A and B in chapter 4.

- *Pellon Craft Fuse*—lightweight interfacing. Freudenberg Nonwovens, Pellon Division, 3440 Industrial Drive, Durham, NC 27704.

Gallery of Grandma's Quilts

The following pages show 11 quilts made by Dena L. Goosman Bockelman. We know that she pieced and quilted at least 17 quilts between 1963 and 1976. Today all of them are owned by her descendants. Nine of her quilts were made specifically for her children and their spouses. The rest were either given away by her or distributed at the time of her death in April, 1977.

Dena used a variety of techniques, including both hand and machine work, to create her quilts. She didn't limit herself to one style. She obviously enjoyed making both the Double Wedding Ring and Grandmother's Flower Garden patterns. She made at least 5 Grandmother's Flower Garden quilts and 7 Double Wedding Ring quilts.

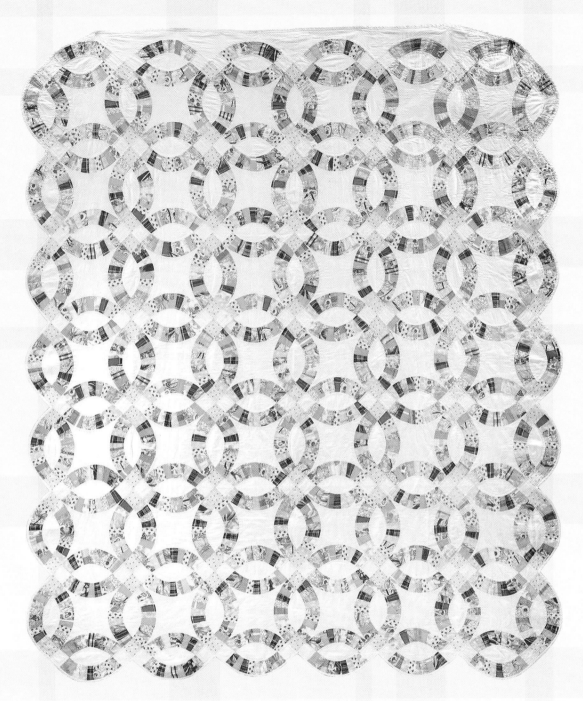

Double Wedding Ring

80" x 90"

Owners: Donald and Audrey Bockelman, Harrisonville, Mo.
This is Grandma's first quilt, finished in January 1963, and is the only one signed and dated.
It has had the most wear of any of her quilts and has worn fabrics throughout. She used her boys' old work
shirts and vowed to never use used fabric again to make a quilt.

Stepping Stones

79" x 93"

Owner: Carol Bockelman, Harrisonville, Mo.

Based on a *Kansas City Star* pattern dated September 9, 1931, this quilt is machine pieced and machine quilted. There is no batting between the top and bottom layers. It is strikingly contemporary with its use of black, red and white fabrics.

Monkey Wrench

77" x 98"

Owner: Carol Bockelman, Harrisonville, Mo.
This quilt is based on a *Kansas City Star* pattern dated January 16, 1929. It is machine pieced and hand quilted.
There is no batting between the top and bottom layers.

Purple Grandmother's Flower Garden

70" x 100"

Owner: Carol Bockelman, Harrisonville, Mo.
This quilt could possibly be the first Grandmother's Flower Garden pattern Grandma made. The blocks, made from 1930s and 1940s feedsacks, were found by her daughter Carol in an abandoned house sometime in the early 1960s near Lake Jacomo, Mo. Grandma set them together with purple for the sashing. It is hand pieced and machine quilted in 45-degree diamond shapes. There is no batting between the top and bottom layers.